# The Absolute Truth About Alcohol & Alcoholism

*J. Logan Duff*

Bloomington, IN  Milton Keynes, UK

authorHOUSE®

*AuthorHouse™*
*1663 Liberty Drive, Suite 200*
*Bloomington, IN 47403*
*www.authorhouse.com*
*Phone: 1-800-839-8640*

*AuthorHouse™ UK Ltd.*
*500 Avebury Boulevard*
*Central Milton Keynes, MK9 2BE*
*www.authorhouse.co.uk*
*Phone: 08001974150*

*This book is a work of non-fiction. Unless otherwise noted, the author and the publisher make no explicit guarantees as to the accuracy of the information contained in this book and in some cases, names of people and places have been altered to protect their privacy.*

*First published by AuthorHouse 8/28/2006*

*ISBN: 1-4259-5098-1 (sc)*

*Printed in the United States of America*
*Bloomington, Indiana*

*This book is printed on acid-free paper.*

This book is dedicated to the ninety-five percent of alcoholics who have been unable to stop drinking; to their spouses, children, friends and employers who have suffered along with them without understanding why or how it happened; it is also dedicated to the civic minded people who are concerned about this escalating social problem and finally, to the citizens, news media, advertising agencies and the leaders of this country who should be concerned.

# Table of Contents

# Introduction

For many years I delayed even attempting to approach publishers with this book for three reasons. 1) I never expected to find a publisher who would have the courage to release it. 2) Most of the present methods for the treatment of alcoholism have reputedly been devised by the most qualified people. 3) The public has been conned, lied to, and so many myths and cover-ups have been created in regards to alcoholic beverages by the alcoholic beverage companies, the advertising agencies, the Federal Government and the medical society, I felt that it would be presumptuous for a layman to assume that anything he had to say on the subject would be taken seriously.

However, the facts show, and statistics prove, that few of the methods of treatment the so-called experts have come up with have succeeded in either curtailing the escalation of alcoholism or increasing the incident of recovery from the disease. And while the true facts concerning the dangers of alcohol and alcoholism are readily available to anyone who will take the time to look for them, the powerful alcoholic beverage business lobbyists, the advertising business, the publishing business and news media make these facts known in such a subtle manner, they have no impact on society as a whole. We have seen in recent years the birth of a multibillion-dollar alcoholic treatment business that has, thus far, failed to do much other than make a lot of people rich. Therefore, I decided to make my contribution to try and help solve this problem with only my own experience, research and the truth as credentials.

This book is the result of over thirty-one years of personal experience as a sober responsible person, after having been an irresponsible drunk, and a great deal of thought and research. I have had hundreds of gut-level conversations with people of every race, creed and color from all walks of life whose lives, in some way, have been dramatically affected because they, or a family member, or a close friend, or a business partner, or a valued employee became either a problem drinker or an alcoholic.

I initially began writing this book because of simply feeling the need to know why I had once been a victim of alcoholism and hoping to discover a solution to prevent the problem from reoccurring. However, the further I progressed into the research it became apparent that I felt <u>compelled</u> to write this book. And it is written with the hope that it might be of help to some of the ninety-five percent of alcoholics who have not recovered from alcoholism, to the problem drinkers who are on the verge of alcoholism and to the families, friends and employers of these people, who have little understanding of why and how their loved ones became problem drinkers. Further, there now seems to be a renewed interest in alcoholism by a number of socially conscious people, without a drinking problem, who are simply aware and concerned about this rapidly escalating, social stigma.

I realized that in order to establish credibility, I would be forced to recount and recall some of my own painful experiences with alcohol, such as remembering how my attention span had become so deteriorated and limited that when a well-meaning friend or family member gave me literature pertaining to alcoholism, it went completely over my head. The majority of this available material was, and remains, filled with so much medical, scientific, religious, psychological and philosophical jargon that, even now, I still find it so incomprehensible and so boring it fails to hold my attention.

When I finally set about to outline this book, I decided that it must be short, concise, informative, written in layman's language and, above all, for a chance to be useful, it must tell the absolute un-sugarcoated truth and not be boring.

Although not meant to be a catharsis on "How I got sober," I will, from time to time, refer to my personal experiences only to establish that "I've been there and done that," but I promise the reader that the summation of my own experience as an alcoholic will be short and sweet.

My experience with drinking alcohol began at age seventeen and progressively worsened until eighteen years later, I became completely dependent upon alcohol. Sober, I was a quiet, conservative, family oriented man, somewhat of a loner. But when I drank any kind of alcoholic beverage, I turned into this totally alien being, without feeling, without compassion, and without fear. Drunk, I could lie, cheat, drive like a speed demon, and fight like a tiger, none of which I could do sober. I became a loud-mouthed, flamboyant extrovert when, in reality, I was a quiet introvert.

Because, when intoxicated, I could shed my normally shy disposition, and could sometimes do more creative and difficult tasks, I actually began to believe I was a better person drunk than sober.

After a brief experience as a party and social drinker, I became a solitary and secret drinker. I became so adept at hiding it, few people were aware that I even had a problem. I kept bottles of booze hidden in my car, my home, and my work place, which I sipped on throughout the day, disguising the odor with mouthwash, expensive after-shave, and cologne.

In the beginning, the alcohol actually enhanced my ability to work long, hard hours and continue to maintain an active home and social life. But after ten years of daily drinking, I began to make mistake after mistake in my business and personal affairs without even being aware of the shambles I was making of my life. Sometimes, when I exceeded the limit of what I needed to get me through the day, I would go on binges. Often, submerging into complete blackouts and disappearing for days. I would sometimes become sober in strange surroundings, in cities far from home, with no earthly idea how I got there.

I finally came to realize that I was allowing my addiction to destroy my life and the lives of the people who loved me and cared about me. With this realization, I began to try, with increasing desperation, to stop drinking for my family's sake and to save my career.

I first tried every conceivable religion, expecting God to miraculously cure me overnight. I was baptized twice while "drunk as a skunk." I then tried several medical doctors, without telling them I had a drinking problem. They prescribed tranquilizers for my nerves and sleeping pills to help me sleep. One even suggested that I drink three or four beers each night, before going to bed. Next, I tried group therapy and personal counseling and finally, Alcoholics Anonymous. Nothing I tried worked for more than a short period.

Then, one fateful day, I decided I wanted to quit drinking for ME, because I deserved a better life than the hell I was living in. Once past the divide, I discovered that I wanted more than merely to be sober. I wanted the freedom to go where I pleased, and to associate with whomever I pleased, without limitations. I also wanted to be strong enough to face up to any situation, without needing a crutch. It was a lot to expect, but I knew that anything short of that type of sobriety would not be enough for me.

I took my last drink on March 9, 1975, at age forty-five. At first, it seemed as if I had been in a coma for ten years. During subsequent years of sobriety, I have found that I remember more of what happened during my intoxicated escapades than I thought possible, things I thought and hoped had been permanently removed. And I've been forced to face up to them and deal with them cold sober. In addition, I have experienced far more traumatic situations, disappointments and tragedies than I ever did as a drunk and have remained clean and sober.

I have not taken any special medication. Except for a brief first year involvement with AA, I have had no contact with any group or organization for the treatment of alcoholism. Finally, I have received no therapy or counseling of any description, nor do I belong to any support groups because of my different views.

At seventy-six years of age, I am still active and in better mental health, than at any time in my entire life. When I choose to do so, I am able to attend parties, weddings or any other social events and celebrations, where other people are drinking, without either taking a drink or desiring one. I can attend sporting events, racetracks, and casinos and remain cold sober. I can travel on airplanes, drive long distances, and converse with people on any level without being fortified with booze. I can attend business meetings and even funerals, without the need or desire to take a drink. I use mouthwash, after shave and cologne that contains alcohol without it triggering an urge to take a drink. Most importantly, I am able to remain in a creative business where pressure, criticism, rejection, and disappointment are the norm, without allowing it to bother me enough to fall off the wagon.

I owe the enduring nature and the quality of my sobriety, to learning the facts that came to light, while researching this book. I do not believe in easy, instant cures. I do, however, believe profoundly in people's ability to heal themselves of most illnesses. If they are informed of all the true facts, in an understandable manner, and If they consider these facts with an open mind and act upon them with a belief in their own ability to succeed.

I made the decision to drink. I made the decision to stop. I began to drink, simply because I liked the false feeling of well being and invincibility I got from drinking alcohol. I became addicted because I continued to drink and not because of any genetic predisposition, chemical imbalance, or deep psychological problem. I quit drinking, because I got sick of my dependency on a drink that turned me completely against my nature. When I eliminated the drink, I eliminated the problem. It's that simple.

I've been clean and sober for thirty-one years! Therefore, I believe that anyone else can do it too!

J. Logan Duff

# Chapter 1

## SOCIETY NEEDS DRUNKS

When I pick up a package of cigarettes and read the Surgeon General's warning about the hazards of smoking, or when I hear the daily criticism and doomsday predictions of smoking cigarettes, it makes my blood boil. I want to shout, "How about whiskey, and wine and beer?" I wonder how many people, including the Surgeon General, have ever compared the statistics of how many people die from cancer and lung disease due to smoking cigarettes to the number of people who die from heart, liver, kidney, brain diseases, and cancer, caused by drinking alcohol? And how about the people who die in automobile accidents caused by intoxicated drivers? Or the ones killed in violent crimes committed by people under the influence of alcohol? Does smoking cigarettes cause people to kill and commit crimes?

1

Between 1982 and 1993, 266,291 deaths in the United States were alcohol related---one fatality every thirty minutes. That is over four times the fatalities suffered in the wars in Vietnam, Desert Storm and Iraq, combined!

There were more than another 300,000, injured in crashes where police reported that alcohol was present.

In 1994 approximately 1.4 million drivers were arrested for driving while under the influence of alcohol or some other drug. These facts are well documented if not well known.

After discovering these shocking and terrifying statistics, I have to ask how is it possible that we're making such a big deal out of cigarette smoking while alcoholic beverages remain legal, inexpensive, easily obtainable and even socially acceptable.

Now there is an ongoing extensive campaign by non-smokers to create a smoke-free environment all over the country. In no way do I deny that this is a good cause. But I have to wonder how many of those involved in this campaign drink alcoholic beverages? When you compare the harm created by both substances, it is unbelievable that so much time, effort and money has been spent informing people about the harm and danger in cigarette smoking and ignoring the problem of alcohol!

How can they even single out cigarette smoking as causing lung cancer and other respiratory diseases, when the very air we breathe is so polluted by the poison from chemical plants, oil refineries and a zillion cars burning fossil based fuel? So why don't these advocates for smoke free air expend as much time, money and energy toward a campaign for pollution free air?

As for myself, I began to both smoke and drink alcohol at age seventeen. When I consumed alcohol in any form, I became both a physical and mental basket case. Now sixty years later, although I have continued to smoke, I have never in my life had a common cold nor have I ever had the flu which proves my lungs are in pretty good shape. And I have no blood pressure or cholesterol problems. In no way am I suggesting that people should not stop smoking and I mention it only to demonstrate why I think smoking to be a minor social problem, compared to the harm created by consuming alcohol.

There was recently a story on the evening news stating that a group of doctors had made a study that showed small quantities of alcohol taken each day, might be beneficial in preventing heart disease. It also stated that some doctors were reluctant to prescribe this treatment because alcohol caused liver disease and cancer. Does it make sense that doctors would be afraid to prescribe something that people can buy anytime they choose and as much as they choose, without a prescription? And if doctors know alcohol causes liver disease and cancer, why don't they inform the public the same as they have suddenly informed them about the harm in smoking cigarettes?

The word "absurd," according to Webster's dictionary, means, "contrary to reason or sense; illogical, with the element of the ridiculous." Absurd also has many synonyms, including "foolish, irrational, ludicrous, senseless and unreasonable."

"Absurd," is, therefore, the most appropriate word I can think of to describe an existing condition that is the most ridiculous, foolish, irrational, ludicrous, senseless, and unreasonable situation in the history of this nation! And I, for one, am very angry about it. I'm very angry that I allowed my addiction to alcohol rob me of what should have been the best and most productive years of my life. Everyone in this country should be very angry that people are allowed to distill and brew alcoholic beverages, without regard for the harm they create. They should also be very angry that the advertising media is allowed to create ads that would entice a saint to drink, but leave out the fact they are advertising what, for some people, is canned and bottled insanity. They should be very angry that liquor stores, bars, night clubs, restaurants, grocery stores and convenience stores, are allowed to sell alcoholic beverages to the public without knowing or caring what happens to the buyer. They should be even more angry that the Medical Society is not giving the public the same information about alcohol as they do about cigarettes, prescription and non-prescription drugs. If I had been given this information I might have made different choices. And they should be livid with anger that our government allows this condition to exist, valuing profit above the welfare of the people.

In Webster's dictionary, alcohol is described as being, a colorless, volatile, pungent, liquid, $C_2H_5OH$, derived from fermentation of sugar and starches, used either pure or denatured, as a solvent, in <u>drugs, cleaning solutions, explosives, and intoxicating liquors!</u> It can also be burned as fuel, is used in industry and medicine, and is the intoxicating element of whiskey, wine, beer, and other fermented or distilled liquors. It is also called ethyl alcohol.

Ethyl is described as being; {ether+ -y l} a univalent organic radical $C_2H_5$, a volatile, colorless, highly flammable liquid $C_2H_5)_2O$ prepared by the reaction of sulfuric acid and ethyl alcohol; it is used as an anesthetic and a solvent for resins and fats.

Most people are aware that ether is an anesthetic used to create anesthesia. Anesthesia is described as being without feeling; complete or partial loss of sensation and sensibility caused by disease or an anesthetic; it is also described as artificially produced unconsciousness or local or general insensibility to pain.

Anesthetic is described as, being without the ability to feel, without emotion; relating to anesthesia; inducing anesthesia, lacking emotion and insensitivity; an agent that causes unconsciousness or insensitivity to pain.

The bottom line is that wine, beer and whiskey contains ether which is why booze anesthetizes pain.

It does not remove the pain. It only temporarily produces the unconsciousness and insensitivity to it.

Alcoholism is defined, plain and simply, as a chronic diseased condition of one who habitually drinks alcoholic liquor to excess, which should make it perfectly clear to anyone that alcoholic liquors are addictive and when a person over-indulges they will become addicted.

Both prescription and some non-prescription drugs produce the same temporary insensitivity to pain as alcohol, doctors will verbally warn a patient about prescription drugs being addictive and both prescription drugs and non-prescription drugs come in containers with a printed warning that continued use may cause addiction. They do not say if you have low self esteem, or a chemical imbalance, or a genetic predisposition, or a defect in character they will cause addiction, the reasons we have been led to believe are responsible for alcoholism. It is simply taken for granted the ingredients cause the addiction. In addition, they carry a list of possible harmful side effects.

Why then is there not a label on alcoholic liquors informing people of these facts?

It is estimated there are between twenty and twenty-five million people in the United States, including between five and eight million teenagers, who are addicted to alcohol. However, as the very last thing the majority of problem drinkers on any level will admit, is the fact that they even have a drinking problem, we can safely conclude there are many more than on record.

Even if the estimates are true, since 1965, the number of alcoholics in the United States has increased over three hundred percent. Yet, the recovery rate remains the same as it was in 1965. In spite of all the supposedly sophisticated new methods of treatment, only five percent of alcoholics ever recover from the disease.

Over thirty-four percent of automobile accidents involving fatalities, and a large percent of the violent crimes, are attributed to perpetrators who are intoxicated by alcohol or other drugs. Alcoholics and other Drug Addicts and their victims, fill our hospitals, sanitariums, asylums, jails, prisons...and cemeteries.

Alcohol is a dangerous and addictive drug that has caused as many deaths and maimed bodies as some of the wars we have fought. These facts are well documented if not well known; yet alcoholic beverages remain legal, inexpensive, easily obtainable and even socially acceptable. Why?

The answer is simple...the economy of this country needs people to drink alcohol. The alcoholic beverage industry and associated businesses have become such an enormous part of our economy, that prohibition, or even a vast reduction in the consumption of alcoholic beverages, would result in nationwide financial chaos. Therefore, although they may be condemned by religion, cursed by society and condescended to by their fellow man, this country <u>needs</u> drunks.

While the distillers and brewers of alcoholic beverages are vested in a multibillion-dollar industry, they are by no means the only ones who need drunks.

The hundreds of thousands of employees of the distilleries, wineries and breweries, need drunks.

The wholesalers and distributors of alcoholic beverages and their thousands of employees need drunks.

The over thirty-five thousand, licensed liquor stores and their hundreds of thousands of employees, who sell over seventeen billion dollars worth of liquor, wine and beer a year, need drunks.

The thousands of bars, night clubs and restaurants, and their hundreds of thousands of employees, whose majority of profit comes from alcoholic beverages, need drunks.

The tens of thousands of grocery and convenience stores who employ hundreds of thousands, and sell billions of dollars worth of alcoholic beverages a year, need drunks.

The multibillion-dollar, alcoholic treatment business, which has sprung up in the last decade and it's thousands of employees, needs drunks.

The multibillion-dollar, advertising business and its employees, supported in a large part by the alcoholic beverage business, needs drunks.

It is hard to estimate when you consider the grain, sugar, and grape growers, the bottle and can manufacturers, the paper manufacturers, the printers, the alcohol manufacturers, and all of their respective employees. But a safe estimate would be anywhere between two and a half to five-million people are employed, either directly or indirectly, by the alcoholic beverage industry and they all need drunks.

Even the United States Government, who collects billions of dollars in taxes from the alcoholic beverage business and income taxes from their employees, needs drunks.

If people stopped drinking, the need for law enforcement officers would be reduced dramatically. The same is true for the judicial departments of government. There would be a reduced need for judges, lawyers, court workers, jailers, prison guards, etc.

If there were a massive reduction in the consumption of alcohol, the hospitals, sanitariums, asylums, and undertakers would all be affected. Medical doctors, along with psychiatrists, psychologists, therapists, and marriage counselors could be fighting each other for patients.

A dramatic decrease in drunks would take a toll on automobile manufacturers, wrecker services, body shops, and insurance companies.

I am pointing out these facts, which are available to anyone who will take the time to look them up, to demonstrate why the escalating problem of alcoholism and a solution, is not too high on many priority lists. Especially, not in a society where the accumulation of wealth has become more important than the welfare of it's people.

The news is filled with scandalous news about illegal drug dealers buying off police officers, judges, bankers, etc. Yet, because of their advertising dollars, sponsorship of sporting events, and their large contributions to charitable organizations, we allow the alcoholic beverage industry, to flourish with little opposition. The alcoholic beverage industry is free to use all media to advertise at will. They employ the very best advertising people to create ads aimed at the youth market and then hire the handsomest men, the most beautiful women, sports stars, movie stars, and celebrities of all types, to give credibility to ads that depict drinking booze as being fun and in a broad sense, sexy. With advertising dollars as bait, the alcoholic beverage industry has largely neutralized the media as a truthful source of information about alcohol and the harm it creates. Except for a few vanilla public service ads, aimed mostly toward drunk drivers, the media does little to warn people of the dangers of drinking alcohol. The Food and Drug Administration now requires all foods, prescription drugs and non-prescription drugs, to carry labels stating all of the contents and warnings as to the possible harmful side effects. If a drug proves to be more harmful than helpful, they jerk it off the market and outlaw it. However, in spite of the known harmful effects of alcoholic beverages, there is not, nor will there ever conceivably be in the future, a label on booze bottles and cans stating their entire contents, or all of the possible harmful side effects. The liquor lobby is just too strong for that to happen.

We are dazzled by the brilliance of the advertising that entices people to drink and we are baffled by the baloney that focuses the blame of wrong doing, on the drinker, and down plays the harmfulness of the drink. We see the public service ads, like the "Know when to say when", "If you drive, don't drink", and "Friends don't let friends drive drunk" insinuating, that it's okay to drink, just don't drive when you drink, or don't let a friend drive. They don't say the reason you shouldn't drive, is because alcohol scrambles your brain, impairs your sense of reason, anesthetizes your feeling and eliminates your conscience to the point, where you don't care about yourself or anyone else.

Why can't people be properly informed about alcohol, just as they are about any other harmful drug. Doesn't the public deserve to be informed of the true contents of alcoholic beverages and warned of the possible dangers and side effects? The primary purpose of this book is a wake up call toward general education so that informed choices can be made. And to, hopefully, help alcoholics and their loved ones understand why they became victims of alcohol and what they can do about it.

# Chapter 2

## WHY PEOPLE DRINK TO EXCESS

The question most asked, by every person involved with an alcoholic, and the question alcoholics most ask themselves, is why they continue to put themselves through what becomes a living hell? Ask people why they drink to excess and the answers will be so numerous and so varied, that they could, (and do) fill volumes of books. But if you carefully examine the answers, it is clear that while they may initially have begun drinking in order to feel <u>good</u>, after long periods of continuous drinking and subsequent addiction they drink in order not to feel <u>bad</u>. To quote the old cliché: "They drink to feel no pain."

Alcohol is no different from most other addictive drug, in that its primary function is to produce the unconsciousness and insensitivity to pain and people experience pain in many different ways, on many different levels, and for many different reasons. People also have different thresholds of pain. What may be extremely painful to some people, will barely affect others. But there is hardly anyone who doesn't experience some kind of physical or mental pain. Pain and fear go hand-in-hand. Pain produces fear...Fear produces pain. Both pain and fear can stem from something of a physical nature, or it may spring from a mental state, such as shyness, over-sensitivity, and fear of death, fear of life, and fear of the unknown. For whatever reason and on whatever level, the pain and fear can become excruciating.

A doctor will prescribe tranquilizers for mental pain and pain killers for physical pain. In both cases they will prescribe drugs that produce an unconsciousness and insensitivity to pain. However, they will only prescribe these drugs on short term and will warn a patient these drugs are addictive and not to be taken for long periods of time. The patients will also be warned the drugs may produce harmful side effects.

What people are not told is that alcohol is the same type of drug as the ones prescribed by doctors for pain. In fact, a large portion of the population is not even aware that alcohol is a drug because they have not been informed of the fact. Alcohol is mostly advertised as a recreational beverage not much different than a soft drink. Therefore, when people discover that alcoholic beverages provide a readily-available, fairly inexpensive, and socially-acceptable, way to anesthetize pain and fear, is it such a great mystery why people use them? Especially, when there is no warning to possible harmful side effects.

The problem is, that people can and do become seduced by this false feeling of well being and invincibility, and desire to remain in that state all of the time.

Another problem is that in order to produce unconsciousness and insensitivity to pain, the drugs that accomplish this must anesthetize <u>feeling, all feeling!</u> The drugs do not separate the good and bad feelings. And when people take these drugs, not only do they become insensitive to their own pain, they also become insensitive to the pain of others. Thus, when people feel no pain, have no regard for others, feel no guilt or fear of reprisal for their actions, they become potential monsters, capable of breaking every law of man or nature, without even certain knowledge of what they have done. Under the influence of alcohol, people have and do commit hideous acts and crimes that are completely against their nature, without even being aware of their actions.

What makes this fact so frightening is that the actions of <u>all</u> intoxicated people are unpredictable. Occasional drinkers, who drink to the point of intoxication, can become just as irrational and unfeeling as the worst alcoholic or illegal drug addict.

Alcohol is a mind-changing chemical. Anyone, with or without a history of drinking, undergoes a personality change after a few drinks. When the things people most fear suddenly become no threat, their personalities can flip-flop. A normally, introverted person, can become an extrovert. A normally, inhibited person, can become uninhibited. A normally, sexually prudent person, can become a sex deviate. A normally, cowardly person, can become a fierce fighter. With all feeling anesthetized, a normally, rational human being, can suddenly go mad. And this turnabout can happen to people, whether they drink every day or just get drunk one time. There is no such thing as a rational drunk, no matter what their reputation or outside appearance. Their brains have been scrambled by alcohol and they are dangerous. If a pharmaceutical company sold a non-prescription drug that affected people as quickly and dramatically as alcohol, they would be crucified by the Food and Drug Administration, the news media, and have law suits out the kazoo.

Isn't it frightening to think there are at least twenty-five million people in this country who, every day, drink to the point where they have no feeling or compassion for their fellow man and have no fear of the consequences of their actions? And there are millions of periodic drinkers, occasional drinkers, and even first time drinkers who may at any given time, reach the same point of intoxication. When you add to that number, the millions of illegal drug users, who are equally dangerous and unpredictable, it really becomes terrifying. When these facts are considered, it is small wonder that crime in this country is getting beyond control.

A "monster", in Webster's dictionary, is described as being an animal, plant or thing that departs from the customary course of nature from its kind. It is further described as being an ugly or cruel person.

Who departs more from the nature of its kind than an intoxicated person? What is uglier than an intoxicated person? What is crueler than an intoxicated mugger, or wife-beater, or rapist, or child abuser? Intoxicated people can and do become monsters.

For whatever reason people begin to drink, if they drink on a continuing basis, they will become addicted. Alcoholism is not class conscious it has no ethnic boundaries, nor age discrimination. Anyone can become addicted. They might possibly occasionally become addicted because of their environment, or because of genetic predisposition, or because they have a chemical imbalance. But mostly they become addicted because they drink alcohol continually and allow themselves to become seduced by the need to feel no pain.

Hospitalized people, even after a very short stay, sometimes become addicted to pain-killing drugs, especially after sustaining a painful injury, or after having a serious operation. People with painful illnesses, such as arthritis, migraine headaches, or cancer become addicted to pain-killing drugs. People accept the fact that if you use opium, heroin, cocaine, marijuana, even prescription drugs, for more than a few times, you will become addicted to them. They are also resigned to the fact, that one can become addicted to tranquilizers and sleeping pills. Why then is it so hard to accept that people become addicted to alcohol, because alcohol is a pain-killing drug? Why is it that when someone becomes addicted to alcohol, they look for a deep psychological or genetic reason to blame the drinker instead of the drink? Is it because, you don't need a pusher or a prescription to buy alcohol? Or, is it because of the fact that we have not been informed that alcohol is a pain-killing, addictive and dangerous drug? Most people even think that alcohol is a stimulant, when actually it is a depressant.

While it is true, that in some instances, having a few drinks might have a therapeutic value, just as prescription drugs do. But, in determining how much is safe would have to depend on many factors, such as a person's size, their physical condition, their frame of mind, whether or not they had eaten before drinking, and the alcoholic content of the drink, etc. And who would take the responsibility of making such a determination, and stand responsible in case their determination was wrong?

Doctors take the responsibility for prescribing prescription drugs, and will warn you that prescription drugs can become addictive and have possible harmful side effects. In addition, they will only prescribe them on a limited basis. Then how come they won't take the responsibility of prescribing alcohol? Even non-prescription drugs carry warnings of possible harmful side effects, however, hardly anyone warns people that alcohol can become addictive and has harmful side effects. And there are no limits on how much you can buy. Does a Bartender or Liquor Store Owner, or a Waiter, or a Store Clerk, give people any type of warning? Shouldn't people who drink alcohol, be entitled to the same warnings that are available on other drugs?

The Media and the Press give much time and space to illegal drugs and drug addiction. The Government spends billions of dollars combating illegal drugs. And this is great! However, there are millions more alcoholics than there are illegal drug addicts. And few seem to be aware that the alcoholics are just as sick, just as uncaring, and just as dangerous, as the illegal drug addicts are. The truth is, alcohol is a drug and alcoholics are drug addicts. There is no difference. Both alcoholics and illegal drug addicts are seeking a way to remove their pain.

People become involved in all types of cults because they no longer wish to have any responsibility or even to make the most trivial decisions. They readily surrender all of their possessions in order to escape responsibility. Alcoholics retreat from society in the same manner, wanting no responsibility, wanting to make no decisions, and wanting to feel no pain. Once they have reached the point of addiction, they cannot allow themselves to feel anything. Any type of honest feeling will cause them pain, whether it is the feeling of failure or success. When they fail, they drink to keep from feeling overwhelming, depression. When they succeed, they drink to keep from feeling the euphoric, sense of success. Having shunned all responsibility, having made no decisions, having not met and overcome any obstacles, they have built up no resistance whatsoever to pain, they cannot bear the slightest feeling.

Alcoholics do not drink to feel good. They drink to keep from feeling anything at all.

# Chapter 3

## WHY PEOPLE BECOME ALCOHOLICS

Since I began seeking insight into what has become the mystery of alcoholism, I have read hundreds of books and articles supposedly written by experts. Many of the so-called "experts" on the subject were so far from accurate; some of their statements seemed as absurd as the condition itself. But nothing I have ever read, seen or heard was as ridiculous as a government funded documentary, aired on public television, wherein an attempt was made to prove that alcoholism was primarily the result of genetic predisposition. It may be reasonable to assume a mother who drinks during pregnancy might pass her own alcoholism to an unborn child. But it is ridiculous to call genetic predisposition the primary cause of alcoholism, when anyone, regardless of race, ethnic background, social position, sex or age, can become addicted to alcohol simply by consuming it on a continuing basis.

During my brief association in AA along with my subsequent years of research, I have met all types of professional people who became alcoholics. I'm talking about doctors, lawyers, judges, priest, reporters, actors, musicians, writers, policemen, and business people of every description, both men and women who'd had it all, intelligence, social status, talent, and wealth. Very few of them attested to having had alcoholic parents. In fact, most of the people I have met in my lifetime, that had never consumed any type of alcoholic beverages, were the ones with alcoholic parents. They didn't drink because the experience with their parents had turned them against drinking, altogether.

Many of our nation's leaders, from the oldest most respected families, were and are alcoholics. We've even had a couple of Presidents who were alcoholics. They didn't become alcoholics because of their genes. They did become alcoholics because they drank too much at social functions and affairs of state, and to relieve the pressure of their offices. Some priests can and do become alcoholics simply because they drink so much ceremonial wine. The theory of genetic predisposition being the main reason for alcoholism just doesn't wash.

People change in every aspect when they drink, because alcohol is a mind-changing chemical. When they cease the use of alcohol, they will revert back to being the person they were before alcohol changed their personality. Therefore, it is the drink and not the drinker that is responsible for the change. Think about it, when people become addicted to tranquilizers, pain pills, any prescription drugs, illegal drugs, even cigarettes, the blame is attributed to the substance. When someone becomes addicted to alcohol, the person who drinks is considered at fault. What has always amazed me about the hundreds of people I have talked with, are the reasons they, give for becoming alcoholics. Even they blame their own inadequacies, the actions of others, their parents, their disbelief in God, or else they are still searching for some deep, dark, unknown source, they can blame, which demonstrates how much we have been brainwashed by the alcoholic beverage industry to believe alcohol addiction is somehow the fault of the drinker. Hardly anyone blames the drink.

The many alcoholics I have interviewed and talked with have given so many reasons, opinions, and excuses for their alcoholism that it would take ten books to record them all. However, practically all of them blamed their own weaknesses and circumstances, rather than the continuing consumption of alcohol. They felt that fixing their personal problems would somehow eliminate their dependency on alcohol and they could drink sensibly.

Another interesting fact is that practically every one of them mentioned their failure to accept what seemed to be the majority of people's concept of God and religion, as a major contributor to their alcoholism. They had either been frightened by the angry God and burning hell of some religions. Or they had been confused and disappointed by the loving, instant miracle-producing God, of others. The ones who were frightened by the angry God, felt they never had, nor ever could, come up to the expectations therefore they felt doomed no matter what their actions. The others, never having felt the presence of the loving God, and never having been the benefactors of any miracles falling out of the sky on them, felt they had, for some reason, been excluded. Therefore, they felt themselves to be terrible people and also doomed.

A great many of them expressed confusion at the existence of so many different churches and religions, each one claiming their doctrine to be the true doctrine, while condemning all the others. They experienced further confusion by the hypocritical behavior of some of the staunch supporters of these religions, who talked one way but acted in a completely different manner. Most of the alcoholics had at one time professed a belief in God, when they didn't truly believe, just in order not to appear different. They actually believed, and some of them had been told, their skepticism about God and religion as a whole was the reason for their alcoholism.

I could have conjured up a good case against God and religion for my own alcoholism. I was raised by a devout Southern Baptist mother who demanded that my siblings and I go to church every time the doors were opened. As a child, the preacher's always loud sermons about an angry God above us and a leaping, burning hell beneath us, terrified me. Later on, I worked in religious television as a director and producer and produced several religious television programs for so-called, healing Evangelists, who were well known and claimed a direct pipeline to God. Yet, I never experienced a spiritual awakening in their presence and never witnessed a single "miracle healing", which I felt to be legitimate. In fact, some of them I knew to be staged. I have ghost written books for some of these Preachers and Evangelists who never even contributed so much as an idea. Yet while claiming to be servants of God, they were perfectly willing to accept credit for being the creator and author of books they never saw until they were finished. It became very confusing.

But my confusion about God and religion had nothing to do with the beginning of my alcoholism. I began drinking steadily, shortly after I became a salesman. I was no more suited to be a salesman than "Ned in the third grade". At that time, I was too shy and too honest. I had been raised to fear God, and love country, in that order, and above all, to be honest and truthful. When I entered the business world I found to my dismay that honesty and truthfulness were not necessarily desirable qualities in some businesses. I also received the rude awakening to the fact, that in order to make a living, you sometimes had to bend the rules. As a retail salesman, I hated lying to people when my company's method of bait and switch advertising, brought customers flocking into the store for what they thought to be a bargain only to find the advertised item was no longer available but they could buy a more expensive one. I also didn't think it to be fair that wealthy people, who were able to pay cash for their purchases, could buy things cheaper than poor people, who were the ones who really needed to save money. When I discovered a few drinks could mask my guilty feelings about such things, drinking alcohol helped me to become top salesman in the entire store. When I advanced into management, I became the one who made up the ads. As I moved up the corporate ladder, the alcohol I consumed at business lunches, parties and social gatherings, added fuel to the flame for awhile. Then there came a point and time when that type of drinking was not enough. So I became a solitary daily-drinker and shunned social drinking altogether. Soon I had progressed into a daily drunk. Finally, I became completely dependent on alcohol.

Being a salesman didn't cause me to become an alcoholic. I didn't have to be a salesman. I chose to drink because it enabled me to subdue the feelings of guilt I felt for being untruthful and dishonest. Masking my guilt with alcohol enabled me to stay in a business I couldn't have tolerated otherwise. If I had known I was drinking a dangerous drug that I would become addicted to and would all but ruin my life, I have no doubts I would have chosen a different career.

Regardless of their religious, social, educational or ethnic background, I discovered a common denominator in the majority of alcoholics I have known or interviewed. Most of them had at one time been extremely intelligent, sensitive, and creative people. The sensitivity that made them feel so intensely, care so deeply, and was the root of their creativity, sometimes also set them apart from their fellow man. Their intelligence sometimes caused them to question things that the majority of people could accept without question. And their intelligence also caused them to attempt ventures others deemed impossible and would never attempt. When their thoughts and actions made it apparent they were different from others, they began to feel there was something wrong with them. In order to fit in, they had a tendency to go to any length to gain acceptance, even to becoming completely phony. They discovered that alcohol could aid them in keeping up this charade. I've seen it happen to people from all walks of life. When the families, friends and employers of alcoholics can be interviewed even though they may have become completely alienated, they will, in almost every instance, attest to the fact that before becoming drunks, their spouses or friends or employees, were good, hard-working, loving, people. Incredibly, some people never seem to understand the change was caused by the alcohol. They tend to believe that a normal person can drink at anytime and as much as they choose without becoming habitual drunks like their loved ones. They think their loved ones became problem drinkers because of some flaw in their character. And that's exactly what the alcoholic beverage industry would have you believe. And while in some instances it may be possible, in the majority of cases it simply is not true!

Even when people stop drinking, turn their lives around and revert back to being the same type of person they were before becoming alcoholics, their alienated family and friends still can not seem to accept the alcohol as being the villain.

While it is true, that people with a high level of self-esteem and self-worth, are probably less likely to become addicted to alcohol, it is also true that even they, if they drink often enough and long enough, will become addicted, which reverts back to the many rich, famous and powerful people, who are and have been alcoholics.

While some alcoholics may first begin to drink just to have fun, others start drinking to anesthetize some pain or fear which is too much for their sensitive natures to endure. When they find out that it works, they develop a tendency to turn to alcohol in any type of a situation that makes them uncomfortable.

Any physical pain can also become of great concern to potential alcoholics. Not really wanting to know if their physical pain is caused by a serious illness, instead of consulting a doctor, they drink to kill the pain, thereby quieting the fear.

After a while, alcohol becomes the answer to everything for alcoholics. It enables them, when there is a need, to walk among their fellow people, without feeling inferior or different. On the other hand, it enables them to draw apart, without needing human contact. They can block out physical pain by drinking to oblivion if need be. Intoxicated, they feel no need for spiritual stimulation, they feel no guilt, no remorse, and they have no sense of responsibility. Soon it reaches the point, where even minute periods of sobriety, will bring all of the feelings that haven't been dealt with, boiling to the surface. Only now, these feelings are more intense and unbearable than before. It is pure unadulterated hell. No one can possibly understand the terror and the pain unless they have experienced it.

When alcoholics need a drink, just like other drug addicts, they will do anything to get it. They will beg, lie, steal, cry crocodile tears, and promise anything. They will prey on family, friends, relatives, casual acquaintances, anybody, for loans and handouts, until they alienate everyone they have ever known.

The tragedy is that these people are not some alien beings. That bum on skid row was once a college professor, or an author, or an engineer. That physical wreck in the charity ward of the county hospital was once someone's beloved wife or husband. That psycho in a straight jacket at the state hospital was once someone's faithful friend. That prison inmate was once someone's loving, mother or father. That body in the pauper's grave was once someone's much loved son or daughter. They all had the same problem. Although no one held a gun to their heads and they had a free will and a choice to do otherwise, they made the mistake of using alcohol to subdue what to them had become unbearable, pain. And they became addicted to what is a dangerous, pain-killing, addictive drug.

Maybe, just maybe, if they had been truthfully informed about what they were consuming and properly warned about possible dangers and side effects, they may have chosen differently.

# Chapter 4

## DRUNKS ARE INSANE

In researching this book, I very carefully selected information from sources that are available to anyone who will take the time to look. And information that can, for the most part, be verified by anyone who has ever been addicted to alcohol or has, in any way, been involved associated with an alcoholic. For obvious reasons, I do not expect verification from the so-called experts.

Although, up to this point, I have made what many people may consider some pretty rash statements, I have said nothing that cannot be backed up with facts. Now I really have a shocker for you. I believe that <u>all intoxicated people are insane and what's more, I can prove it!</u>

If you doubt this statement, pick up Webster's dictionary or Roget's thesaurus and read the definitions of insanity. A few of the many definitions of insanity are; to be out of one's mind; to lose one's senses or reason; to lose one's faculties or wits; to take leave of one's senses; to lose one's head; to go mad; run amuck; to rant, rave and dote; to drivel; to hallucinate, etc.

The worst of the insane people are the ones classified as having psychopathic personalities...the sociopath, the delusional maniacs. The psychopathic personality is a person whose behavior is largely amoral and asocial and who is characterized by irresponsibility, lack of remorse or shame, perverse, impulsive and often, criminal behavior, and other behavioral defects. The sociopath is a psychopathic personality whose behavior is aggressively, antisocial. The maniac, is a wildly or violent insane person; a madman; a lunatic. Depending upon their degree of intoxication, ANY of these definitions can apply at one time or another to the behavior of an intoxicated person!

Every day, people open their homes, schools and businesses to spouses, children, relatives, friends, students, and customers, who are intoxicated. Due to the personality change that has taken place because of their intoxication, some of these people are just as insane, just as unpredictable, just as potentially dangerous, as the inmates in the violent ward of an asylum. They are without reason because they are incapable of rational thought. They have no compassion because they are incapable of feeling.

They are dangerous because they are without fear of reprisal.

If you don't believe this to be true, just pick up your local newspaper or listen to the news on radio and television.

Every single day, someone is killed or maimed by an intoxicated driver.

Every single day, someone is raped or mugged by an intoxicated rapist or mugger.

Every single day, an intoxicated robber holds up a business.

Every single day, men, women, and children, are beaten, abused, and even killed, by intoxicated spouses and parents.

Every single day, an intoxicated employee causes an industrial accident.

Every single day, people go into bars, attend social events, business meetings, sporting events, and after a few drinks wind up arguing or fighting with each other or some other patron. Sometimes someone is killed.

Every single day, homes are broken and divided because of drinking.

Every single day, partnerships are dissolved and businesses go bankrupt because of drinking.

Are drunks insane? Of course they are, and not just alcoholics but anyone who drinks alcohol to the point of intoxication. Wouldn't people have to be out of their minds to speed recklessly on today's busy freeways without being in complete control of all their faculties? Those "Friends don't let Friends Drive Drunk", ads are a joke. Did you ever try and stop a drunk from driving? Without fear, they think they can drive better drunk than sober.

Wouldn't people have to have taken leave of their senses to beat up and abuse their spouses and children?

Wouldn't any person who went against his own nature and acted in an irrational, irresponsible, totally unfeeling manner, be considered insane? And who can argue that drunks don't rant and rave and dote and drivel and hallucinate? A psychotic person is described as having no feeling, no compassion, no fear, and no guilt. Neither do intoxicated people, as long as they remain intoxicated.

Nobody could ever succeed in convincing me that I wasn't insane when I was drinking, I know differently, especially, in the later years. Even though, thankfully, I never physically abused my family, my actions in other areas were nothing short of insanity. I became involved in the music business and as the Garth Brooks song states; "I had friends in low places". I went to places to visit some of these friends, where even the police were afraid to venture. And to places even I wouldn't have thought of going, cold sober. I went to Harlem in New York, the Watts area of Los Angeles (a week after the riots); Little Havana, in Miami, the ghettos in New Orleans, and never gave a thought to the danger of an intoxicated small, white guy, alone and unarmed, venturing into such places. The people I visited were always surprised by my visits and were afraid <u>for</u> me. I have been all over New York City, San Francisco, Los Angeles, Las Vegas, Nashville, Chicago, Miami, New Orleans, Dallas, Philadelphia, Washington D.C. St. Louis, Kansas City, and Houston, nearly always alone and the majority of the time so drunk I was out of my mind. I have awakened in sleazy motels and hotels in many of these cities with no earthly idea how I got there. These facts, alone, would be a good case for insanity, but that's not the worst of it.

I am not a hunter because when I am in control of all my faculties, I can't bear to kill animals of any kind. I would surely never even think of harming another human being. However, during my drinking years, again I have to say, especially in the later years, I was not only a potential murderer I was a potential <u>mass</u> murderer. On a given day, depending upon my degree of intoxication, I could have lined up all the people who I felt were my enemies and mowed them down with a machine gun and never given it a second thought. Every alcoholic I have ever shared with confessed to having the same type of thoughts, one time or another. After having been sober for many years, it is inconceivable to me that I could have ever harbored such thoughts.

When I see public service announcements, such as the one showing an egg frying in a pan to demonstrate how illegal drugs effect the brain, I think about my own craziness and I wonder what the people who produce and pay for these ads think <u>alcohol</u> does to your brain? Alcohol, not only fries your brain, it pickles it.

Many people tend to believe that the majority of fatal automobile accidents are caused by drivers who are alcoholics when actually it is the so-called normal people who drink to the point of intoxication who are responsible. The normal business people coming from a business meeting or social event where they had too much to drink; the intoxicated normal high school or college student coming from a prom or party; the intoxicated wife or husband who have had an argument with their spouse; the normal career people who stop for a few drinks after losing their job; the normal people in stressful jobs who toss a few to relieve the pressure; the normal politician who becomes disillusioned with the system, and needs a drink so he can rest his mind. These are the people who cause most of the automobile accidents caused by drunk drivers. The majority of people who have become alcoholics don't even own a car. Or, if they do, they more than likely do not have a driver's license.

The truth is, there is no such thing as a normal sensible drunk!

And what about the date rapes, bar fights, fights at sporting events? Aren't most of these incidents caused by so-called normal people who just had too much to drink?

If you are still not convinced that drunks are

insane, then visit the psycho ward of any charitable or veteran's or military hospital and see how many of the inmates are there because they are suffering from the delirium tremors, or hallucinations brought on from drinking alcohol. Go to the state insane asylums and see how many of the inmates are there because of alcoholism. I say go to these places, because most alcoholics can't afford treatment in private sanitariums or the plush alcoholic treatment centers. If you still have doubts, visit the jails and prisons and see how many of the inmates are there because of crimes they committed while intoxicated.

If you have a drinking problem of your own and are not convinced that you are insane when you are intoxicated, then examine your own actions, thoughts and behavior. Then see if you can truthfully tell yourself you're not insane when you're drunk.

If you're a spouse, relative, or friend of a problem drinker, you can't possibly know your loved one's thoughts but you can examine their behavior and actions. Are they the actions and behavior of a sane, rational, human being? I think not.

I know what drinking alcohol did to me. It assassinated my character, it changed my personality, it numbed my feelings, and it seduced me into a false sense of well being, while my body deteriorated and my quality of life dwindled toward oblivion. I don't care if every celebrity, movie star, and sports star in the world, says a certain beer tastes great and is less filling, I know that for me, it's really bottled and canned insanity. And if any distiller of whiskey, or brewer of beer, or maker of wine, or any other alcoholic beverage manufacturer, gave me a guarantee, written in blood, authenticated by the Surgeon General, signed by all members of the Supreme Court, and witnessed by the President and the Pope, that they manufactured an alcoholic drink that I, or anyone else, could drink to the point of intoxication without  temporarily becoming an insane creature without feeling, without compassion, and without fear, I would not believe them. Not for one second.

# Chapter 5

## ALCOHOLICS VS. DRUG ADDICTS

Usually, people think of alcoholics as being in a different category from drug addicts. When in truth, alcohol <u>is</u> a drug and alcoholics <u>are</u> drug addicts.

Alcohol is a mind-changing chemical, the same as marijuana, cocaine; opium, heroin, etc. are mind-changing chemicals. Alcohol is addictive, just as other drugs I've mentioned are addictive. Granted, cocaine, heroin, and opium are more powerful, so it may be assumed that addiction can occur faster. But addiction is addiction, whether it occurs fast or slow. Besides, drugs such as cocaine, heroin, and opium, are much more difficult to obtain than alcohol because they are much more expensive and they are <u>illegal</u>.

The important fact is, there are many more people addicted to alcohol than to <u>illegal</u> drugs. Also, the number of casual and occasional users of <u>illegal</u>

drugs is only a fraction of the number of casual and occasional drinkers of alcohol. Illegal drugs, are not nearly as great a threat as alcohol because, it is against the law to keep illegal drugs in your home and serve them to guests. Illegal drugs are not sold in the majority of grocery and convenience stores. While there are no corner illegal drug stores, there are plenty of corner liquor stores. Illegal drugs are not advertised in newspapers, magazines, and on radio and television. Illegal drug dealers do not sponsor television shows, sporting events, and make magnanimous contributions to charity. No illegal drug dealer has twenty-five thousand trucks on the highways delivering their products, as the president of a beer company was quoted in a national magazine as saying his company had. Illegal drug dealers, and their employees, do not pay billions of dollars in taxes.

Because they pay taxes and make all kinds of public service and charitable contributions, should that give distillers, brewers, and wine makers anymore right to sell harmful, addictive drugs to the public, than the illegal drug dealers? Evidently it does! A good example of how far the establishment goes to sugar-coat the dangers and harm in alcohol, is the difference in how drug dealers and pushers are depicted in movies and television programs, compared to the way alcoholics and people who sell alcohol are depicted.

The drug users are always shown as mean, desperate, and crazed people, who have become hooked on drugs by force, making the drugs the heavy. These depicted addicts, will go to any lengths, killing, robbing, lying, cheating, even turning on their own kind, in order to get a fix.

The drug dealers are always depicted as cruel, ruthless, automatic-weapon-toting, psychotic killers, who mow down civilians and cops alike, in order to protect their turf. And this is probably a true picture.

On the other hand, alcoholics are usually depicted as weak, unfortunate people, whose bad luck in love or misfortune in business, or defect in character, turned them into the friendly, neighborhood wino, who wouldn't harm a fly. But ask the cops in any big city, how many winos get knocked off every year in battles over a cheap bottle of booze or wine. Ask them how many people get killed and mugged by alcoholics who need money for a drink. A few years back, a man in Texas was executed for murdering a convenience store operator, for a lousy six-pack of beer. If they can't hold a job and they've alienated everyone around them, where do people think those twenty to twenty-five million alcoholics get money to buy booze?

Bartenders and liquor storeowners are nearly always depicted as friendly, fatherly types, who you can tell your troubles to and who will cut you off when they think you've had enough to drink. If you can find any bartender or liquor storeowner who will listen to a drunk babble about his troubles for over two minutes, I'll nominate him for the humanitarian award. Further, if you can find a bartender or liquor store owner, who even cares how drunk you are, as long as you can pay for drinks, I'll buy them a few drinks.

It makes absolutely no difference what the drug is, when people are addicted to it, there is nothing they will not do, in order to obtain it. They may be completely different in social position, race, creed, color and age. Their preference in drugs may vary. But when they are intoxicated, by whatever drug they may take, drug addicts are all the same. They have no feeling, they have no compassion, they have no fear and they are dangerous.

When addicts are without the drug of their choice, they are also all the same. Everything and everyone is a threat to them and they are a threat to themselves and everyone.

Even though people in authority know these facts about alcohol, they will never be widely publicized in the way the harmful effects of illegal drugs or cigarettes have been publicized, because of the economic repercussions.

Isn't it amazing that it took over two hundred years of people smoking, for the Health Department, the Medical Society, and the Government to discover that smoking can be harmful to your health? And isn't it ironic that the great vendetta against tobacco came about shortly after Greenpeace began to harp on factories, chemical plants and refineries for polluting the air until it was causing all types of respiratory diseases. Then suddenly the blame for these respiratory ailments shifted to people smoking cigarettes and the threat of air pollution became a minor problem in the public eye.

The establishment now readily states that nicotine is a harmful, addictive drug. They even accuse the cigarette companies of inserting large quantities of nicotine into the cigarettes in order to make them even more addictive. But does smoking cigarettes change people into monsters, who rob, steal, maim and kill? How many people die young because of smoking cigarettes? In these days of frivolous lawsuits for enormous sums of money, how come if cigarettes are so harmful, and it can be proven, why aren't people suing the cigarette companies right and left? And, if they are so harmful how come cigarettes are still on the market? Why doesn't the Medical Society demand they be taken off the market? They may not sell as many cigars and cigarettes as they once did but they charge four times as much for them so they don't have to sell as many to still make a huge profit. And the government collects four times more taxes. I keep referring to cigarette smoking because the news is full of the steps being taken to stamp out smoking altogether. So why don't they just take cigars and cigarettes off the market like they've done with the prescription drugs that have been proven harmful? Could it possibly be that some deal has been struck? And why is it that the Medical Society and the Government are so adamant about warning people of the dangers of nicotine but do little to warn people of the dangers of alcohol, which is a much more harmful substance?

Could it be because they're afraid if the judicial system admitted that intoxicated people were temporarily insane, every inmate in custody for committing a crime, while under the influence, would file for a new trial and plead they were temporarily insane when they committed the crime. And every person, who intended to commit a crime, would get drunk first expecting to be exonerated.

There is no simple solution to the problem of alcoholism, as complete abstinence is the only cure. And if people want to drink, they're going to drink. We've already found out that prohibition will not work in this country. For if you try and tell free people in a democracy, they can't do something, they will find a way to do it in spite of everything. But it is imperative that we find some alternatives. For if we consider the number of alcoholics, the illegal drug addicts, the borderline alcoholics and addicts, the potential alcoholics, and addicts, the occasional drinkers and users, and the social drinkers and users, on any given day, half the population of the United States could be insane.

A drug is a drug is a drug...

# Chapter 6

## WHY THE RECOVERY RATE IS SO LOW

Because people are deluded when intoxicated, they are able to function with pain and situations that would make them dysfunctional, sober. Therefore, because they can continue to function, they may begin to think they are better people drunk, than sober.

In the beginning, drinking alcohol may enable shy or timid people to come out of their shells and become more aggressive. After a few drinks, the serious and somber people may loosen up and suddenly become very amusing. Even their families, friends, and associates, may, in the early stages of their drinking, find them more pleasant and amusing to be around when they are drunk.

Artistic people, such as artists, musicians, actors, dancers, and writers, are constantly striving for perfection in their art. They are usually their own worst critics and are seldom satisfied with the results of their efforts, causing them a great deal of mental anguish. Many of them live in a state of constant fear of being replaced and losing status if they fall short of perfection in their work.

Athletes and performers of all types, have the same perfection bent. These types of people are especially susceptible to addiction, because intoxicated; they become less fearful and critical of themselves. They may begin to think they perform better intoxicated, than they do sober.

Regardless of the circumstances, as long as people suffer under the delusion they can do anything better drunk, than sober, therefore making them better people, it is almost impossible for them to recognize their drinking as a problem. Thus, they can become seriously addicted, long before they come to a point where the addiction is recognizable to others.

The families of alcoholics, often unknowingly, contribute to their addiction. Out of shame and embarrassment, they close their eyes and their minds, to the possibility of their spouse or child having a serious drinking problem. They lie for them, cover up for them, and coddle them, when they should be holding them responsible for their actions and demanding they seek help. They succumb to the false promises, the crocodile tears and lies of their addicted loved ones, instead of taking a firm stand and sticking to it. They continue to pity them and give them compassion when they should be giving them a kick in the butt. Surprisingly, the majority of alcoholic's loved ones continue this type of behavior until the alcoholics do something terrible enough to completely alienate the loved ones. And the facts prove they <u>will</u> do something against their nature. If people become addicted to alcohol and do not stop drinking or seek help, statistics show that they will commit a crime and wind up in jail or prison, or they will go insane and be committed to an asylum or sanitarium, or they will die, sometimes violently, often by their own hand. A sad future for anyone, but especially sad, for people who are often gifted and talented and have everything to live for.

Unfortunately, alcoholics seldom recognize the need to seek help nor will they seek help, until the pain, fear and guilt, become so great, they can no longer be anesthetized. At these times, alcoholics find themselves in the precarious position of neither being able to get drunk, or to get sober. It is a terrifying experience.

When the majority of alcoholics I have talked with reached this point they, as I did, sought help through religion. Like most people who abuse their minds and bodies, one way or the other, they went searching for, not necessarily the miracle of instant cure, but for instant relief. I have heard of alcoholics losing their craving for alcohol overnight during some type of religious service or ceremony and I, in no way, question that this might not be true. But in all my experience, I never personally met the benefactor of such a miracle, nor have I ever met anyone who personally knew someone who experienced an overnight healing. Unfortunately, for this notion, of all the people who at one time or another try to counsel people with drinking problems, it is my opinion that clergymen, unless they are recovered alcoholics themselves, are the least qualified to do so.

Outside of the street preachers, and the self proclaimed messengers of God in Evangelism, the majority of clergymen in Organized, Fundamental Religion, have been brought up in the church. Most of them entered the ministry directly from college and the seminary, with very little living experience of their own to draw from. Their colleagues throughout life are usually other ministers and the members of their own religious organizations. Clergymen may be well versed on the Bible and have great theological knowledge however the major portion of their time is directed toward the affairs of the church and to its members and supporters, as it should be. Most of them have a tendency to look at life in terms of Christians and sinners, good and evil, with nothing in between. In short, they are mostly inexperienced with the seedy side of life which, in my opinion, makes them unqualified to identify with, or to offer counsel to fragile, complex people, like alcoholics.

When alcoholics go to clergymen, suffering from bad hangovers, sick, nervous, scared, perhaps filthy and smelling bad, most clergymen have no earthly idea how to even communicate with them. More than likely, the clergyman will try to get rid of them as quickly as possible, with the facile assurance that he will pray for them.

The absolute, hardest thing that alcoholics ever do is to admit they <u>are</u> alcoholics. While they may have no qualms about asking or even begging for money or booze, they can hardly bear to ask for any other type of help. So usually, the clergymen they approach for help have no conception of the effort it took for alcoholics to ask him for help. Few clergymen are aware that most alcoholics have been searching for and praying to God most of their lives and have been unable to find Him or to reach Him. So when the clergymen give them the standard answer that all they need to do is pray to God and ask that they be cured, assuring them God will do just that, it can be devastating if it doesn't happen.

During that crucial first period, when alcoholics ask for help, a more knowledgeable person may have been able to help. Due to the ignorance of the clergymen, it will probably be a long period and maybe never, before those alcoholics seek help again.

Hardly anyone seems to understand that when an alcoholic reaches the stage of not being able to get drunk or sober and seeks help, he is not at that time seeking a cure. He is seeking something other than alcohol to stop his pain because alcohol isn't working anymore. Only a person with knowledge of alcoholism will recognize this and know what to do. They will recognize this condition will only last for a short time. And if the alcoholics don't find a substitute quickly, they'll go back to alcohol. And the next time, it probably will work. Thus, they'll fall back into the same old syndrome\ until alcohol fails them again.

Doctor Carl Jung, arguably the greatest of modern day psychiatrists, was completely baffled by alcoholics, and stated the only thing that appeared to help them was a spiritual or religious experience.

Alcoholics baffle medical doctors, psychiatrists, and psychologists unless the doctors, etc. happen to be recovering alcoholics themselves. Treatments for all manner of illnesses are based upon the doctor's own experience, theory, case histories and what the patients themselves tell their doctors. But the thing alcoholics fear most, besides being without booze, is confinement. Therefore, alcoholics, who usually trust no one, lie to the doctors, psychiatrists, and psychologists. They usually only consult them to get temporary relief from pain. And quickly learn just what to say in order to get other types of drugs, painkillers for pain, tranquilizers for nerves, and sleeping pills to make them sleep. The doctors cannot successfully treat them because they are not told the alcoholics true symptoms.

Because of their own denial and the denial of their loved ones, alcoholics are usually severely addicted before anyone realizes it. No one seems to recognize it, until their social graces become so deteriorated, their behavior becomes socially unacceptable. By the time this happens, they have usually alienated their families, friends, and several employers. They may have already committed a crime, caused a terrible accident, or even been institutionalized.

In short, before alcoholics admit they need help, or seek help, or are forced to seek help, they are almost beyond help, at least by conventional means.

Is it then any wonder why the recovery from alcoholism is so low?

To add to the dilemma, hospital space is at a premium and very expensive. State mental hospitals, Veterans hospitals, and charitable institutions are over crowded and understaffed. Private sanitariums and alcoholic treatment clinics are beyond the means of the majority. By the time most people have succumbed into alcoholism, few have families, or anyone who even cares about them. Few have careers or jobs, a great many have criminal records, and are unemployable.

We continue to build more prisons to hold the rapidly escalating number of criminals, yet take few proactive measures to stop crime. We make few attempts to educate and rehabilitate prisoners, so upon release, they can return to society as useful, productive citizens. We continue to pass harsher punishment for lawbreakers, yet do little to assist them to not become lawbreakers. We manufacture, advertise, and sell what can be harmful drugs to our citizens, yet when they become insane we either punish them, or turn our backs to them and ignore them altogether.

It has been my intention to paint a bleak and disturbing picture of the escalating problem of alcoholism, because that's what it is. And if it continues to increase at its present rate, the recovery percentages do not improve and more preventative measures are not taken, twenty years from now, the majority of American citizens could be alcoholics or other drug abusers.

Examine these facts and even look up the statistics for yourselves. Then ask yourselves if this situation is not the epitome of absurdity!

# Chapter 7

## THE MYTHS OF ALCOHOLISM

Although medical science has discovered and developed miracle drugs and preventative vaccines, to treat and prevent diseases which have plagued mankind since the beginning of time, they would have us believe they have not found an answer to the escalating problem of alcoholism. They have developed techniques whereby they can transplant lungs, hearts, eyes, livers, and kidneys, and yet they would have us believe they have found no way to improve the low recovery rate from alcoholism. They have invented patches that supposedly help people to stop smoking, why can't they come up with something similar for drinkers? Smokers are considered just normal, ordinary people who became addicted to tobacco because the manufacturers of cigars and cigarettes inserted more nicotine into tobacco unknown to the innocent smoker, thereby making it more addictive and making the product at fault. On the other hand, even though alcohol is also an addictive substance, the establishment would have us believe that some people can drink alcoholic beverages continuously without becoming addicted. These people are referred to as normal. The person, who becomes addicted to alcohol, does so, because of some defect in their character, or physical make-up, or their genes, which makes them abnormal. The truth is that whether normal or abnormal, anyone who indulges in any addictive substance on a continuing basis will become addicted to that substance. It is also true that the only cure for addiction of any kind is abstinence.

Although they are quick to condemn the situation, neither Organized Fundamental Religion, the New Age Religions, nor the so-called Faith-Healing Evangelist, have been able to slow the growth of the problem of Alcoholism. Neither have they managed to increase the rate of recovery.

The lawmakers, while ever continuing to inflict harsher punishment on lawbreakers, have had little effect on either decreasing the number of people who cause automobile accidents, commit crimes, or just foul up while intoxicated, or increasing the number of people who seek treatment and recover.

Medical science is inclined to blame the increase in alcoholism on psychological make-up, genetic predisposition and chemical imbalance, but have done little to find a solution to the problem.

Society blames environment, racial, sex and religious discrimination, television, motion pictures and even the sexual revolution, for the increase in alcoholism.

Religion blames man's departure from God, the influence of the devil, and man's natural sinful nature, for the escalating number of people who become alcoholics.

Virtually no one blames the alcoholic beverage companies, the advertising agencies, or the media who run the ads. But the truth is, it is impossible to become an alcoholic without consuming the drink on a continuing basis. By the same token, it is impossible <u>not</u> to become addicted if you <u>do</u> drink on a continuing basis. Mankind does and always has had a tendency to complicate simplicity. It is no different with the problem of alcoholism.

History tells us that the Indians first introduced tobacco in this country to the pilgrims. And people have been smoking ever since, for over two hundred years. Yet, only during the last two decades, did the public begin to be informed about the possible harmful effects of smoking cigarettes? Is it possible that in this age of medical miracles, that only recently medical science discovered smoking to be harmful to your health?

So what about alcohol? If a layman like me can gather these facts which are available to anyone and figure out how we are being conned and manipulated by the alcoholic beverage industry and the media, why can't the people who we elect to public office to safeguard our welfare?

Some of the third world countries, such as the Far Eastern and Middle Eastern, countries, the African nation etc., have more social, political, and financial problems than we Americans could ever dream of. Their poor are the poorest in the world. They are exposed to more disease, poverty and death, than we could ever imagine. On the other hand, their rich are among the richest in the world and are involved in more business pressures, political controversies, and financial crises, than we can comprehend. But these countries don't have the problem we have with alcoholism. Why not? The answer is simple. The majority of the peoples in these countries are of the Moslem, Hindu, and Buddhist faith. They simply do not drink alcoholic beverages.

And what about the Jewish people who have suffered almost every negative situation, known to the human race? They have been enslaved, slaughtered, imprisoned, hated, discriminated against, and are to this day vilified by Christians for murdering the Messiah. They are considered outsiders in every country in the world including their own homeland. Yet, there are few Jewish alcoholics or drug addicts. Could it be because Jews are taught from birth that they are God's chosen people and therefore, very special. So, in spite of what others may do to them, say to them, or say about them, they have enough self-esteem and self-worth to withstand any outside adversity and few of them ever use drugs of any kind to mask the pain.

The <u>truth</u> is that blaming <u>anything</u> other than consuming alcohol on a continuing basis for the increase in alcoholism is ridiculous. Poverty does not <u>cause</u> alcoholism; ethnic background does not <u>cause</u> alcoholism; and genetic predisposition, does not <u>cause</u> alcoholism. Drinking alcoholic beverages, which mask and anesthetize feelings, on a continuing basis is the <u>cause</u> of alcoholism. Eliminate the drink and you eliminate the problem.

Unfortunately, while still the greatest country in the world, our present society has fallen short of what our forefathers envisioned for this country. And the majority of us judge each other by astonishing, superficial, basics. People are judged by what they <u>have</u>, rather than by what they <u>are,</u> by their <u>appearance</u>, rather than by their <u>behavior</u>; by their <u>words</u>, rather than by their <u>actions</u>. Money and power are more important to people who have it, than the welfare of their fellowman. This reversal of the principles this country was built upon, has caused a reversal in our thinking. Thus, the alcoholic beverage industry has, through it's manipulation of the media and it's advertising, flooded us with so much misinformation about alcoholism, it has managed to lay the burden of guilt for alcoholism on the drinker, rather than the drink. But if you examine all the facts, this misinformation doesn't hold water.

For instance, their drinking aside, alcoholics

are the same people they were before they became alcoholics. Though the alcohol may have temporarily pickled their brains and they may even have forgotten, they still have the same talent and ability to create and the power to rejuvenate they have always had. Sober them up, detox them, build up their physical and mental strength and you'll find people who are still decent and useful human beings. We have a great many important, powerful and useful people, who are recovered alcoholics.

When I see documentary films, read books, articles and reports assigning the cause for alcoholism to anything other than the continuing consumption of alcohol; I am skeptical of the credibility of these studies. Who funded them? And who were their subjects?

Doesn't it seem strange, that in spite of all the expensive studies by scientific organizations, in spite of all the elaborate sanitariums and alcoholic treatment centers now in existence, and in spite of all the different religions, cults, churches and healing evangelists, the organization credited with having the greatest degree of success in the treatment of alcoholism, is Alcoholics Anonymous? Yet, Alcoholics Anonymous is a self-funded, self-governed, self-contained, anonymous organization. How can it possibly have more success than other organizations, some of whom have state-of-the-art facilities, which are well funded and staffed with professionals?

Could it be because the people who belong to

and lead AA are recovering alcoholics themselves, who, having experienced the hell of alcoholism really <u>care</u> about helping other alcoholics to get and remain sober? Or is it because AA has no fees or dues? The only requirement for membership is a desire to stop drinking.

Another reason for AA's success could be because AA is usually the last resort when alcoholics bottom out and are ready for a change. They may even have been sent there by some judge as an alternative to jail time. But for whatever reason they first go to AA, more alcoholics stop drinking and begin to recover in AA than any other support group.

However, even in AA, where there are supposedly no rules or regulations, there are twelve steps which must be addressed in order for AA to work, thereby creating a way of life. The alcoholics, who are able to embrace this new way of life wholeheartedly, can and do recover. But even though AA's success rate is higher than any other method of treatment at this time, it is the minority, rather than the majority, who accept it.

Let me here reiterate. The five percent of alcoholics who have found a way to stay sober should stick with it, no matter what it is. But alcoholics are difficult to treat, at least by conventional means because they have no self-esteem and have lost their ability to believe and trust in anyone.

No medical doctor can help a patient unless that patient tells the doctor the truth about his ailments, and then trusts the doctor's method of treatment.

No counselor of human behavior can be of any assistance to a patient, unless the counselor is informed of all of the patient's relevant background and the patient believes in and follows the counselors' method of treatment.

In religion, before a priest can give absolution, before Jesus can take on the sins, and before God can forgive sins, the person seeking redemption must believe it can be done and confess those sins in their entirety.

Unfortunately, the majority of alcoholics fall short of all these requirements in medicine or religion.

Does this then mean that alcoholics, who have lost a belief in themselves, a belief in their fellow man, and a belief in God, are doomed and beyond help? While some would have you believe this is the case, it simply is not so! If it were so, I certainly wouldn't still be here, sober, and writing this book. And I'm living, breathing proof that there is no such thing as a hopeless drunk!

You may be trying to stay drunk until the funeral, because you've lost all hope. But believing you are beyond redemption because of what others do or say, is a huge mistake.

Even if you've lost your family, your friends, your reputation, all of your material possessions, and your self-respect, there is still hope for you.

Even if you're an agnostic or even an atheist, there is still hope for you.

No matter what your physical or mental condition, as long as you're alive, there is still hope for you. And you are worth saving! Because you still have what you've had since the day you were born, the ability to think and reason, the ability to create, and the ability to rejuvenate. Most importantly, because you are still alive, in spite of your lifestyle, you have the will to survive!

Get up right now and look into a mirror. If you don't have a mirror handy, then look into anything that will show your reflection. Take a good long look. Maybe you don't like what you see. Maybe you don't like what you've done to yourself. Well, let me tell you, regardless of how you may have abused your mind and body and regardless of what deteriorated state your body and mind may now be in, you are looking at a marvel of the ages. You are a living, breathing, human being, the most complex life form on this planet, and as far as we know, in the universe. What's more, you are a unique, human being. In the entire universe there is not another one exactly like you.

Of all the inventions made since the beginning of time, no machine, no matter how intricate, is as complex or as magnificent as you are. No computer ever built has your ability to think. No spacecraft has your power to reason. And no other life form has your capability to create and rejuvenate.

Regardless of your past, the real you, the inner you, is no better or worse than any other human being on the face of the earth.

During your lifetime, you have touched lives and altered circumstances that you are not and will never be aware of. And you're not through yet. There is a purpose in your still being here that has not been fulfilled or you'd be dead.

Though your body may now be badly deteriorated and ravaged by alcoholism, with proper diet, medication, exercise and determination, it can be regenerated into a strong, healthy body.

Though your mind may now be clogged and befuddled by your abuse of alcohol, by study, concentration, and mental exercise, you can clear up your thinking and old skills and talents can be relearned.

Though your material possessions may be long gone, they can be replaced through your skills and talents, and by your own creations.

However, you must <u>want</u> to regain your skills and talents. You must <u>desire</u> some material possessions. What is more you must be <u>willing</u> to pay the price.

To do it the way I discovered, you will not be required to join any organizations. You will not have to attend any boring, repetitious, meetings. There are no rigid rules and regulations that must be adhered to, except you must stop drinking alcohol. The only belief you'll need is a belief in yourself. Unless you're very sick physically, you will need no medication. You can set your own pace and you can do it alone. However, your rate of recovery will depend on your desire to get well, and your willingness to act. There will be no cost or fees other than the price of this book..

Regardless of all the myths that exist about alcoholism, the majority of which have been conjured up to cover up the harmful effects of alcohol, there are simple explanations for the problems and simple ways to eliminate the problems. Although simple, they are not easy. I've eliminated the problem in my life. I'm hoping this book will help you understand your alcoholism and will assist you in eliminating it from your life.

# Chapter 8

## WHAT ALCOHOLICS CAN DO FOR THEMSELVES - BY THEMSELVES

While sharing thoughts and experiences with hundreds of alcoholics and reflecting on my own experience, I found with many of them, including myself, there were four factors, besides the obvious physical discomfort, that had blocked, or were blocking, our attempts to stop drinking. These factors were: 1) our lack of self worth; 2) the guilt we felt for our past actions; 3) the anger toward people we felt had wronged us; 4) and the fear of what the future might hold for us. These feelings of worthlessness, guilt, anger, and fear, surfaced during brief periods of sobriety and were so excruciatingly painful, they had to be vanquished immediately which, of course, called for more booze.

No doctor, or psychiatrist, or psychologist, or counselor, or preacher can possibly understand the excruciating pain, the humiliation, the feeling of complete isolation, the feeling of hopelessness, the terror, and the depth of the dependency of alcoholism unless they have experienced it themselves. Well, let me assure you that I do know. I have experienced it all...in spades.

If the aforementioned factors are blocking your attempts to make a new beginning, let us take them one at a time and show you what can be done to knock down these barriers with facts.

1. THE LACK OF SELF WORTH: There is not a human being on the face of the earth that is completely worthless. As a human being, you are a part of the whole of mankind and, therefore, are of value. There is a purpose for your being here, even though that purpose may never be revealed to you. The very fact that you are still alive, in spite of your lifestyle, proves that you are a survivor. You've taken all that life has thrown at you and what you have brought upon yourself and you've neither killed yourself, nor allowed yourself to die. The physical abuse alone, which you have subjected your body to, would have been enough to kill lesser people. Besides the illnesses you've, no doubt, brought upon yourself, you may have been beaten up, robbed, raped, cut, shot and even tortured. You may have been in jail, prison, a mental institution, and no doubt subjected

to humiliation far beyond what any human should have to endure. You may have suffered the mental anguish of loss of family and, friends, reputation, all of your material possessions and, most certainly, the loss of self-esteem. But you haven't committed suicide and, miraculously, you are still alive. Few so-called normal people could have endured the hell you have already suffered as an alcoholic. Therefore, you are much stronger than even you realize.

The very hardest thing for me to do when I first stopped drinking was to convince myself that I was even worth saving. Fortunately, I had a wife who never stopped loving me and believing in me. And as I never went home when intoxicated, my children had hardly ever seen me at my worst, so I still had a family. However, former friends, relatives and business associates had been putting me down for so long that I had begun to allow their opinions to govern what I believed about myself. And what others said or thought about me was not nearly as bad as the thoughts and beliefs I had about myself. When I began to realize that I had survived all that without completely caving in, it gave me enough feeling of self-worth to continue on. It proved to me that I had a purpose for being here or else I would already be dead. And I became curious to try and find that purpose. Aren't you in the same boat? Aren't you curious to find out why you have survived?

Look at it this way. You've probably already lost every thing that was of any value to you. So, what more do you have to lose? What else can life throw at you that you haven't already experienced and survived? The worst thing that can happen to you is that you'll die. But wasn't it essentially, a death wish that caused you to continue to drink? No, my friend, you may think so, but in reality, subconsciously, you have a very strong desire to live. So strong, in fact, that you've put yourself through hell, in order _to_ survive. What you have done is mask the reality of pain you were unable to face up to sober, with alcohol. When you are strong enough to throw your alcoholic crutch aside, because of your strong survival instincts, you will miraculously find the strength to continue to survive, sober. You will no longer need a crutch.

2. GUILT FOR PAST ACTIONS: When you make the decision to stop drinking, from day one, you must become your own defense lawyer, for you are on trial. Not in a court of law, but in your own mind. Maybe people have been telling you how worthless, sorry and irresponsible you are. You surely have been berating yourself. At the moment, you probably believe it to be true. Have you ever thought of yourself as being a victim? Because that's exactly what you are. You are the victim of a drug that alters your state of mind into a false feeling of painlessness and invincibility. Most people become addicted without being aware of it. They became addicted to the insanity that allowed them to break rules and laws and temporarily mask the fear of reprisal of such actions. Maybe you became addicted to the false

courage that allowed you to express your anger at life as a whole, without temporarily feeling the guilt that comes from such action.

Perhaps you have been drinking for so long that you no longer think you can bear to feel even the slightest pain for more than a few seconds. You can bear much more than you think, because you are much stronger than you think. As a unique individual, you have, and always have had, a freedom of will and choice that no person or outside force can interfere with, unless you allow them to do so. It only requires a change of attitude. And before you can begin to regain any semblance of health, you're going to have to make a change of attitude. In fact, in the beginning, that's about the only change you are going to be able to make.

You're going to have to learn to live in the now. This will only be possible when you stop reflecting on the past and worrying about the future. You must realize that you can't change one second of what has already been; neither can you alter one second of what has not yet happened. In spite of one's social or financial position, in spite of their state of mental and physical condition, there are no guarantees anyone will make it beyond this moment, this hour, or this day. Here and now is all you or anyone else has. So you're no different from anyone else in that respect. Also, in the here and now, you have the freedom to live life to the fullest or to your own destruction. The choice is, and always has been...yours. To live in the now, you must learn to accept what is. The alcohol you consumed masked the reality of the now. It did not eliminate the pain, fear and guilt. It only allowed you to believe, temporarily, that they did not exist. Perhaps even to the point where you began to think they had been permanently removed. But you have, no doubt, found when you have had minute periods of sobriety, that all the pain you never dealt with, no matter what the source, is still lurking there waiting to surface the moment you get sober enough to feel it.

When you learn to live in the now, that means moment to moment, hour to hour, day to day, you can learn to suppress that old pain until you gather the strength to want to recall it so it can be dealt with. That is not to say it won't creep up on you unexpectedly, from time to time, but you will learn to realize it is part of the past and no part of the now.

You have probably tried to stop drinking several times for various reasons...for your family, your business, etc. But have you ever tried getting sober just because you want a better life? Well, I've got news for you, my friend, no matter how noble your intentions, until you decide to stop drinking for yourself alone, it is never going to work. Besides, in the beginning, it's not going to matter to anyone except you! The people you've been feeling guilty about hurting, have probably built up such animosity and resentment toward you, they never want to see you again, drunk or sober. Or else they just no longer care about you.

So, it certainly is not going to mean anything to them if you stop drinking. And if you run to tell them you've stopped drinking, you've probably lied to them so much in the past they will not believe you anyway. In all probability, they will not care whether or not you're feeling remorse for your transgressions. You will find that to most of the people you have harmed, both you and what you did to hurt them, just doesn't matter to them any more. And they have probably let go of you, period, which is precisely what you must learn to do with them. Let go of them. That doesn't mean, if sometime in the future, when you're in a position to do so, that you shouldn't pay back money you've stolen or borrowed and never repaid. You need to do that for you and your own peace of mind. But that is in the future and no part of the now. Besides, to be able to live in the now, it is important to recognize that nothing you do will heal old wounds. And don't expect to rekindle old loves or renew old friendships. It sometimes happens, but mostly in fiction.

That is why you must stop drinking for yourself alone because, more than likely, it really will not matter to anyone else. Nothing you do is going to matter to anyone but you, which includes feeling remorse about your past transgressions. Besides, those transgressions are a part of the past and no part of the now. The only things that are going to matter are what you do, think, feel, and say, in the now.

3. ANGER AT PEOPLE WHO YOU FEEL

WRONGED YOU: A common ailment of most alcoholics and even recovered alcoholics is what is known as the "poor ME's." The "poor ME's", reflect the anger and resentment alcoholics harbor against people who they feel have wronged them and who they blame for a great deal of their misery. This anger and resentment is sometimes felt to such a degree, when they're well enough to feel, it can block any attempt to stop drinking. Suppressed anger and resentment are emotions which, when they get beyond control, can cause even sober, rational people, to become irrational and dangerous. Intoxicated people, of any description, who are angry and resentful, are like loose cannons. You can ill afford to have anger and resentment.

You can rid yourself of anger and resentment by recognizing you have, and always have had, a free will and a choice, which means that you chose <u>for</u> you and you are responsible <u>for</u> those choices. In all marriages that failed, in all relationships that broke up, in all business partnerships that went sour, you made the choice for you. No one forced you to love him or her. No one forced you to befriend him or her. No one forced you to go into business with him or her. The favors you did that were not reciprocated. The money you lent that was not repaid. The love you gave that was not returned. These were all choices made by you, for you. You did not have to do any of these things and you could have walked away at any time. They are now history and a part of the past. They are no part of the now. And to dwell on them will only result in creating more harm to you. By the same token, you must realize that the people you've harmed also had the right to not get involved with you. They also could have walked away at any time. So you are not responsible for their pain, or guilt, or anger.

Recognizing that you are a unique individual with a free will and a choice will help you to realize that you and you alone, are responsible for every word you speak, for every thought you think, for every action that you take, and for every feeling that you have. No one else is responsible for what you say, think, do, or feel. This knowledge also relieves you of the responsibility of what others, say, think, do or feel. No matter what you do, you can't change the way others talk about you, think about you, or feel about you. To even try is wasted energy. The only thing you can change is your own attitude to accept what is, in the now.

So if you are responsible for you and everyone else is responsible for himself or herself, how do we forgive each other for our transgressions against each other? By understanding where the responsibility lies and first forgiving ourselves for the harm we've created in our own lives. The people, who you felt harmed you, made a choice for themselves the same as you made a choice for yourself. Either they're sorry about it or they're not. That is not for you to decide. All you can do about it is let it slide into the past where it belongs and forgive yourself for your role. But no amount of reflection is going to change what has already been. Forgive means to forget, to tear up, and to cancel out. It is time to forgive yourself and start living in the now.

4. FEAR OF THE FUTURE: Just as you cannot relive the past, neither can you project yourself into the future. First, you must realize that it is not going to be easy to live in the now and not worry about the future. Human beings are creatures of habit. And old habits are hard to break. But it is possible. You are a survivor and you can take steps to survive the unknown future, just as you have survived the past.

We are not going to cast a magic spell or zap you with a spiritual awakening that will cure you overnight. What we are going to do is supply you with simple facts and logical explanations to help you regain your health and sanity, if you apply them. The action is entirely up to you. Always keep in mind it will probably take as much time to restore your body to a healthy state as it took to deteriorate it to its present state. But that is pure speculation. You may not be as hardheaded or as hard to convince, as I was. The only thing you need to concern yourself with at this time is that it is possible, if you're willing to work at it.

It has always astonished me how many of the alcoholics I have talked with, were idea people just like me. And the majority of them had the same problems with their ideas as I had. I could get an idea and in my mind, put it together, project the outcome, and see the final results, all within the hour. If I was fortunate enough to be able to actually get the idea into production, it drove me to distraction when the people I worked with couldn't immediately recognize where we were going with the idea, without the benefit of an explanation. And I drove them to distraction because as one business partner put it, "I was ten miles down the road while everyone else had stopped for the stop sign, without ever explaining how I got there." If the idea didn't materialize the way I had first envisioned it, I would be devastated. If it did turn out exactly as I envisioned it, I'd still be disappointed. I couldn't understand why I didn't feel more elation about the success. It never occurred to me that I had already felt the elation, way back when I projected the outcome in my mind. I have learned since, that it is okay for me to plan for the future, as long as I don't project the outcome. This is a problem that seems to plague most alcoholics and one of the reasons why I think they have a hard time finding a program that works for them. They project the outcome before they really get started and become disappointed when it does not reach their expectations.

I am assuming that you are an alcoholic who has been unable to achieve sobriety through any of the available treatment programs, or maybe you're sober, but haven't reached the degree of sobriety you'd like to have. In either case, consider this; maybe you, like me, are uncomfortable in a group situation. The member who is least able to comprehend sets the pace of a group. Therefore, if you're a quick study, the pace of the group may be too slow to hold your attention. It may also bother you that some people who become sober through groups, are encouraged to, and do, become solely dependent upon that group for their sobriety. It may bother you as it did me, to be told that in order to stay sober, you must attend meetings and associate only with other alcoholics. In other words, follow certain rules and regulations, when supposedly there are no rules and regulations. To me, it became very confusing and eventually, annoying. I finally decided that if I attended one more boring, repetitious meeting, listened to one more drunkalogue, or heard one more cliché, I'd blow the sobriety I did have. If I had remained in any of the programs I tried, I do not think I would be sober today. By the same token, I once had an alcoholic, writer friend, a Nashville newspaper reporter, who had been sober for twenty-five years. Yet, in order for him to remain sober, he attended, and may still have to attend a group meeting every day of his life. The poor guy could not use after-shave lotion, mouthwash, or anything that contained alcohol, without it triggering the craving for a drink. In his case, a group situation was his salvation.

In some groups, a belief in God or, at least, a higher power is a necessary part of the quest for sobriety. I would be scared to death to even question whether a faith or belief in God wouldn't or doesn't help some people. <u>All</u> of the available programs work for <u>some people</u>. But what if you are an atheist or an agnostic? Are you beyond help? Some people would have you think so, but that is not necessarily true.

If it is impossible for you, at this time, to believe in a celestial being who sustains life and alters circumstances, how about trying a belief in a power inside yourself that has kept you alive when you were trying so hard to do yourself in? Is it so hard to believe that you had an unknown inner strength to withstand all the trials and tribulations life threw at you and a will to survive, which had come from somewhere? Hasn't just the fact that you are still alive proven something to you? How about believing that you alone caused all of your problems and with your own power of reasoning, you alone can find the answers to your problems? One of man's greatest fallacies is looking outside himself for the cause of his problems and looking outside himself for the answers to his problems, when it all comes from within.

You have the power within to heal your illnesses, rebuild your body and regenerate your mental capacity. Any doctor will tell you that a great deal of illnesses lie within the mind. Of all the creatures on the earth, man alone has the ability to reason and create. And you have the power within to create the means to take care of your problems.

All of this power and ability may come from an all powerful, living, loving, God. And according to the Bible and millions of believers, it does. However, you do not have to believe in God, in order to have it. You were born with it. So for the present you just need to use it and not try to understand the source.

When you begin to live in the now, you will realize that life is not all that complicated. It is the human race that makes it so artificially complex. But even in today's complex world, our genuine needs are simple, as they always have been. We need only air, food, water, shelter, clothing and love, in order to sustain a decent quality of life. Anything other than that is a want or desire. And it is our wants and desires that cause our problems.

We abuse our bodies, then, expect instant cures for our illnesses and pain. We put ourselves in situations that are mentally devastating, then, expect instant relief from our misery. When other people can't help us and God doesn't seem to want to, then we try to hide from the reality of the situation, rather than to look to ourselves for the causes and solutions to our problems. A cliché often used is "let go and let God." Even good Christians believe that God created us with a free will and choices that not even He will interfere with. They also believe He gave us everything necessary to sustain life, the power to think and reason, the power to rejuvenate, and the power to create. It is my belief that we need to utilize everything in our own power and expended every effort in our own behalf to solve our own problems before God will intervene.

As an alcoholic, you became the victim of an addictive, seductive drug that allowed you to avoid temporarily the responsibility of your own sometimes cruel words, thoughts and actions. It also allowed you to postpone feeling the pain that comes from such irresponsible behavior. Further, it allowed you to delay paying the price. However, eventually, you will have to pay the price.

As a unique member of the human race, you do not have to drink alcohol in order to survive. Neither do you have to depend upon the opinions and actions of others to stop drinking. You have the power within, to stop drinking, to regain your health, wealth and peace of mind. Consequently, if you've found no other way, you must look within to find the solution for you. Others may share their experiences with you but they are not you. What worked for them will not necessarily work for you. No one else can stop drinking for you. No one else can rebuild the health of your body and your mind. No matter what, you are never going to be like anyone else, because you are unique, as they are unique.

Once you are able to let go of the past, and stop worrying about the future, you will at some point reach the stage of life everyone must come to at least once, known as, "the moment of truth." The moment you realize you are all alone with decisions to be made, only you can make. And the only choice you have is to either help yourself or perish. Even though it is true you are alone, it is also true, that "He is the strongest, who can stand alone."

You must choose between getting sober voluntarily, or wait until you commit a crime serious enough to send you to prison or you lose your mind, or you die. These are the only choices you have. And believe it when I say that getting sober voluntarily, even though it's hell, is a hundred times better than being forced to get sober in a jail, or prison, or asylum or in the psycho ward of some state or charitable hospital.

In essence, I've probably told you a lot of things you already know which is the reason you haven't fit into groups and why repetitious, sometimes boring meetings, haven't helped you. It's probably why religion has not helped you so far. It is probably why therapy hasn't helped you. You have probably always known subconsciously, that in order for sobriety to work for you, you must do it alone, drawing strength from within. You may have always known that you could not be satisfied with a sobriety dependent upon your association with others. Maybe like me, in order for sobriety to work for you, you must be free to associate with whomever you please, and to go wherever you please. Perhaps like me, you needed to know why alcohol turned you into a psychotic lunatic.

You may never again regain your lost wife and family. You may never regain old friendships, business relationships, or lost possessions. But you can regain your sobriety. You can regain your self-respect. You can regain both your physical and mental health. And you can make a beginning this day, this hour, and this moment. Yesterday is gone. Tomorrow is not here yet. This is the now. Learn to make the most of it!

# Chapter 9

## GETTING SOBER AND STAYING SOBER

If my efforts to make this a hard-hitting, no holds-barred book have succeeded, you have been informed with hard, cold, and true facts, that alcohol is a dangerous, addictive drug. You have been informed as to why these true facts about alcohol are seldom mentioned. You have been informed with hard, cold, and true facts, as to why alcohol is sold and will continue to be sold to the public, in spite of these facts. You have also been informed with hard, cold, and true facts that intoxicated people are insane. If that isn't enough to motivate addicted people to stop drinking, how about the hard, cold, and true facts, that explain imprisonment, insanity, or death, as the only alternatives.

If you make the decision to stop drinking, you have several ways from which to choose in order to make a beginning. You can enter a detoxification center and have the alcohol removed from your system. You can enter one of the programs whereby synthetic drugs are used to replace the alcohol. You can try group or one-on-one therapy. You can try for a miracle cure through religion. You can enter a volunteer program such as AA. Or you can quit on your own, cold turkey. The main objective is for you to stop drinking. If you feel medical treatment is necessary, get it. If you feel the need of religious stimulation, seek it. If you feel the need of group or one-on-one therapy, ask for it. If you have tried all of the above and they didn't work, I suggest that you try cold turkey again. And do it for no other reason than you want to do it for you.

When you've put the cork in the bottle, there will be four essential needs to get you back on your feet; nourishment, physical and mental exercise, and some type of work.

At the beginning of your sobriety, depending upon the length of the period you've been drinking to excess, you will probably only to be able to take in small amounts of food. At this time, honey will alleviate some of your misery. Honey is high in dextrose that will give you energy. It reaches the bloodstream rapidly to replace some of the blood sugar that alcohol destroys. Honey will give you a lift when you're feeling shaky. Honey can be taken straight, mixed with milk or juice, poured on pancakes, waffles or cereal, or used as a sugar substitute in all types of beverages.

I have always been a coffee drinker. One of the first remedies I ever heard of for a bad hangover was to drink a lot of strong black coffee. When I made my serious commitment to stop drinking, I briefly tried AA. When I arrived at my first meeting, someone shoved a cup of coffee in my hands. I was to learn that people at AA meetings drink lots of coffee. For eight or nine years into my sobriety, I still drank lots of coffee, especially in the mornings. I also continued to have panic attacks and periods when I got shaky, especially in the mornings. Then my wife developed some health problems and the doctor told her to avoid any food or beverages that contained caffeine. We began to drink decaffeinated coffee. Some time later, it dawned on me that I hadn't felt shaky nor had a panic attack since I began to drink decaffeinated coffee. To this day, as long as I drink decaffeinated coffee, I have no problem. I could have avoided a lot of misery if I'd known this in beginning. Now I'm passing on this information. If you drink coffee, make sure it's decaffeinated.

In addition to honey, drink at least six to eight glasses of water a day and several glasses of fruit and vegetable juices. This will provide nourishment, plus help to clean out your system. When you are able to eat solid food, eat foods that contain a lot of protein. Additional vitamin and mineral supplements, will help build up your stamina, but never try to substitute supplements for food. Instead of eating three large meals a day, eat five or six small meals. This will keep your energy level on an even keel.

In the beginning, the only exercise you should attempt is walking. Begin with short walks, extending the distance each day until you can walk for several miles. Walking in parks or scenic areas will also help you once again to get in touch with the peacefulness and beauty of nature.

Once you have built up your stamina by walking, you may want to try other exercise. In the beginning, moderation is the key slowly adding a little more each time you exercise. Exercise will not only build up your body strength, if you set aside short periods each day for exercise, it will put some discipline back into your life.

Even though at one time, you may have been the Chief Executive Officer of General Motors, you may find after long periods of continuous drinking, that even a minimal job will tax all of your mental faculties. Besides, if you have destroyed your reputation, a minimal job is about all you're going to be able to get at this time, maybe not. Maybe you have the type of career that you can step right back into. The important thing is to not worry about, think about, or talk about, what you once were, or were able to do. That is in the past, just as your bad times are in the past. They do not exist in the now. Concentrate only on what you can do at this moment. Regardless of what you are forced to do to get by, financially, as long as it's honest work, do it the very best that you can and you will find it to be very rewarding. While you're rebuilding your strength, relearning forgotten skills, and regenerating your mental faculties, in many ways you'll feel like a child again.

If your mental prowess has been harmed to a great degree, you're going to have to strengthen your power of concentration. Reading is a great way to rebuild your power of concentration. Up until I became completely dependent on alcohol, I had always been a speed-reader, and had read hundreds of books. I was also a quick study, with almost perfect recall. During my college days, I could go to a lecture and afterwards quote it almost verbatim. Yet, when I first stopped drinking, my concentration and power of retention was so minute, that the only books I could comprehend were children's books. So I began to read children's books. It really wasn't so bad, because in reading children's books, I relearned some of the principles, I had all but forgotten. So if your power of concentration and comprehension has been impaired, go to the public libraries and read anything you are able to comprehend, even if in the beginning it's only children's books. If you can't concentrate enough to read, most of the libraries now provide facilities where you can listen to books on tape. Attend any free lectures that are available, if only to see how much you can retain. Go to church, even if you're a non-believer. Churches are free, and even though you might not believe, you can listen and sharpen your powers of concentration and retention.

Many people, who have stopped drinking for

a short time, will want to run to former spouses, friends and business associates and tell them of their accomplishments. If you are contemplating such a move, be warned that except in rare instances, the people who do this are usually disappointed in the response they get. Remember, if your spouse, or friend etc. doesn't have or has never had a drinking problem, they will have no idea what an effort it took for you to maintain just a short period of sobriety. They probably don't understand why you became an alcoholic in the first place. If you make the mistake of telling them you love them, they won't believe you. Because you must understand that if you've been drinking for a long period of time, you haven't loved anyone for a long time. You haven't even loved yourself and it is impossible to give somebody else something you don't have. Therefore, even though you may be sober, if you have not yet begun to love yourself, others will sense this.

If you're serious about your commitment to stop drinking, now is the time, as never before, to become honest with yourself because it is imperative that you learn to love yourself. Only when you can rekindle the love of self, will you be able to give love to someone else. And that love you have to give is going to be your greatest asset in your fight to get and keep your sobriety.

Once you have begun to strengthen your body and improve your concentration, you need to begin to rebuild your self-esteem. If you're an alcoholic who has stopped drinking, you have accomplished what ninety-five percent of alcoholics haven't done. That alone ought to make you feel pretty good about yourself. And if you're working on regaining some of your strength of mind and body, you can also give yourself a couple of points for that. But the greatest way to build self-esteem is in doing for others, expecting absolutely nothing in return, not even gratitude. The only way you can help others for your own satisfaction is not to hold them in your debt. It is also the only way to avoid disappointment when people are not grateful or don't reciprocate your favors. Further, when you reach the point where you can once again give love, if there are no strings attached to your love, you won't be disappointed if it is not returned. You'll be satisfied that you are once more able to experience love, period.

You must realize by now that we are all victims of businessmen who manufacture, advertise and sell a dangerous, addictive drug without regard for human life. We are also victims of a money-hungry, government, that don't care about us. And we're victims of a society that condones drinking alcohol then puts a stigma on us when we become hopeless, alcoholics.

Doesn't that make you really angry? Doesn't it make you want to do something to stop this insanity? Because if you won't, who will? The entertainment and news media won't do it, because of their fear of losing financial backing, sponsorships and advertising dollars. The medical society and scientific organizations are evidently forbidden to do anything about curtailing alcoholism, because they couldn't help but know the facts about the harmful effects of alcohol.

The alcoholic treatment centers that charge for their services are certainly not going to hand out free information. And outside the medical profession, it is difficult to find people with enough knowledge about alcoholism, to speak out. Even some of the free alcoholic recovery programs, tell their people not to get involved in anything controversial and to not try and help anyone with a drinking problem unless they ask for help. That to me is ridiculous! For who else is better qualified or has the courage to warn people of the harmful effects of drinking and describe the horrors of alcoholism, than people who have either recovered, or are recovering, from alcoholism, themselves? Don't young people with their whole lives ahead of them, and people who are borderline alcoholics, at least, deserve to hear the truth, whether they act on it or not?

Do you want a reason to stop drinking? Do you want a purpose to keep on living? Well, here it is! What better reason than to maybe contribute to salvaging others from the obscenities you have experienced? Here's a job you can do that few people have the desire or courage to do. It is also a means by which you can make restitution to the entire human race for your own past mistakes and irresponsibility.

You can tell people the truth about alcohol and what it does to the mind and body.

The only person who ever believed I could get sober and stay sober, the way I chose to go about it, was me. Now, because I believed and still believe in me, I also believe in you. I believe you can get sober and stay sober in spite of what anyone says to the contrary, and in spite of all circumstances, if only you want to and will. I believe you can, because I did.

But I can't change your attitude. Only you can do that. I can't make you have a belief in yourself. Only you can do that. I can't make you want to get sober and have a better life. Only you can do that. It is as it always has been, entirely up to you, whether you live your life to the fullest or to your own destruction. I can only hope you make the right choice for you.

# Chapter 10

## SOME THINGS TO THINK ABOUT

Within a year, after the massive onslaught on smoking began, cigarette sales declined by eight and a half million packages. Since then, the required warning on cigarette packages, the banning of cigarette commercials on TV, the public service announcements by the Surgeon General, the Heart Association, etc. have been instrumental in causing millions of people to stop smoking. People all over the country have suddenly become familiar with the alleged, harmful effects, of cigarette smoking. Many of these people have become involved in a movement for a smoke-free environment. Even the people, who continue to smoke, have cut down, which proves that when people are informed, whether true or not, in matters concerning their health and welfare, they will listen and respond. THE SAME CAN BE TRUE IN

# THE CASE OF ALCOHOL.

Prohibition was tried in this country and proved to be an utter failure, although it had a host of both defenders and detractors. The defenders claimed it succeeded in reducing deaths, divorces, accidents and poverty. The detractors claimed it fostered an evil far worse than the one it attempted to suppress, because it was impossible to enforce, and provided the criminals who bootlegged beer and whiskey with their main source of income, much the same way as illegal drugs do today. Prohibition failed, because it didn't inform people of anything. It simply prohibited the sale or consumption of alcohol, taking away the right to choose. The economic ramifications were disastrous, and many historians blame prohibition for triggering the events that led to the market crash of 1929 and thus The Great Depression. In addition, because of all the illegal night clubs that provided the thrill of tasting forbidden fruit, it is estimated that more people began to drink the illegal booze during prohibition, than had ever consumed legal alcoholic drinks.

With the modern day liberal mind set that demands a logical explanation for everything, it appears quite evident that prohibition would not work now, just as the laws against illegal drugs have done little to curtail their sale and use. Prohibition and harsher punishment just don't work. Education and information do.

If the government had passed a law prohibiting

the sale and smoking of cigarettes, more people would probably be smoking now, instead of less. But instead, they gave the public the information about the possible harm in cigarette smoking, then left the decision, up to the individual. The impact, while affecting the tobacco industry, has hardly made a dent in the national economy. The same could be true in the alcoholic beverage industry.

There is an organization called MADD, (Mothers Against Drunk Drivers) which has no doubt gathered enough support to trigger the rash of public service announcements about drunk drivers. Their influence has been instrumental in getting Laws passed for harsher punishment for drunk drivers. Some insurance companies are now including the treatment for alcoholism in their health care benefits an issue they would not have considered a few years ago. Concerned parents, becoming more aware of the problem of alcohol abuse among teenagers, are holding meetings to discuss the problem. These steps are a vast improvement over the lack of concern of previous years. But we have far more to be concerned about than drunk drivers. And most of the activity is in after-the-fact measures. There are few pro-active measures being taken.

Those MADD mothers and concerned parents should direct some of their anger at themselves for not being more concerned about a problem that affects all of us, until disaster struck at home.

They also might now want to contact the public

servants who we elect to office, along with the Surgeon General and demand that they give the public the same type of information and warnings about alcohol as they have done about tobacco and other potentially harmful drugs.

If they also directed some of that anger at the advertising agencies that make up the ads, the sports stars and celebrities who star in them and the media that runs the ads depicting drinking as being fun and glamorous, there might not be so many alcoholic teenagers to be concerned about. Young people are far more apt to try a beer indorsed by some major sports star, than smoke a cigarette promoted by a cartoon character like Joe Camel.

Anger directed toward all aspects of the problem, instead of in just one area, might result in reducing not only the threat of drunk drivers but other alcohol-related problems.

The most effective preventative measures for curtailing alcoholism can be put in motion by the people closest to problem drinkers, their families, friends and employers. These people first need to understand that when they coddle problem drinkers, cover up for them, and sympathize with them, they are prolonging recognition on the part of the drinker that he even has a problem.

THE WIVES. When a spouse gets arrested for drunk driving, wives often due to embarrassment or fear, make excuses for their intoxicated husbands, and rush to bail them out of jail as quickly as possible.

Wives call employers and tell them their spouses are too sick to come to work, when they're drunk or have a bad hangover. Wives continue to listen to the lies, the broken promises, and succumb to the crocodile tears, even when they know they are being conned. Wives argue and threaten when their spouses get drunk, then forget all about what they said when the spouse temporarily sobers up. Wives take the children and leave when their spouse come home drunk and abuses them, then return when the spouse sobers up, apologizes, and promises it won't happen again.

If you are a wife and you have allowed this situation to occur more than once, you are not doing what is best for you or your spouse! You are not only jeopardizing the welfare of yourself and your children; you are contributing to the destruction of the husband you profess to love. What you must understand for your own welfare, as well as his, is that, intoxicated, your husband is not capable of feeling. In this condition, he neither loves nor respects you or your children. He is not even aware that his actions are harming you, or does he care. Even though he may not have ever been abusive, that can change instantaneously, especially if you let your anger get out of control and start an argument. Remember that he became intoxicated because something is so painful to him that he couldn't bear it sober. And he is blaming the cause of that pain on something or someone other than himself. This time it might not be you. But if he continues to drink, a time will come when it will be you.

THE HUSBANDS. Husbands, while usually not as tolerant as wives, sometimes make the same mistakes with intoxicated spouses that wives do. Husbands come home from work, to spouses passed out in bed with the housework undone and dinner uncooked. They jump in, clean up the house, fix dinner then tell the children mommy is sick. Husbands lie and make excuses when their wives get drunk and are unable to attend family get-togethers. Husbands sometimes bury their heads in the sand and pretend it isn't true when they suspect their wives of having affairs with other men. Husbands often discount it as their way to relieve pressure, when their working wives habitually stop for a drink with fellow employees after work.

What you must understand is that she doesn't clean the house because the house means nothing to her when she's drunk. You mean nothing to her. The children mean nothing to her. If she is having affairs with other men they mean nothing to her. Intoxicated, she is incapable of having any feelings for anyone.

If you are a husband and you allow the situation to continue, divorce is almost a certainty. The other possibilities are; she may kill herself, you may kill her or one of her lovers, she may do something to harm the children. Any of these situations would be enough to destroy your lives or the lives of the children.

THE PARENTS. Parents refuse to recognize that when their children get into trouble, the possibility of their children having a drinking problem. Parents refuse to believe it is possible for a teenager to become an alcoholic. Parents bail their children out of jail immediately, when the children get arrested for being drunk publicly or driving while intoxicated, then pay the fines for tickets and pay for damages. Parents pay for the special insurance rates in order for teenagers to drive, then, assume the attitude that the insurance company will and should pay for it when their children have wrecks and damage other people's property.

You parents, above of all people, must understand that your normally, beautiful, loving and respectful children, are potentially little monsters when they are intoxicated. Intoxicated, they don't care about rules or laws. They feel no remorse that they wreck your or someone else's car. They could care less that maybe you had to put up your home as collateral for their bonds. They may feel deeply about all of it when they sober up. But if they're alcoholics, they will simply drink until they can no longer feel the guilt and remorse.

THE FRIENDS. Friends unknowingly contribute to prolonging the recovery of alcoholics, by lending them money, co-signing for loans, even carrying booze to them when they are unable to get it for themselves. They are as susceptible to the promises, the lies and the crocodile tears of their alcoholic friends, as the families are.

THE EMPLOYERS. Employers also unknowingly

help to prolong the agony of alcoholics, by giving them several chances after frequent absenteeism or just plain fouling up on the job.

All people who care about alcoholics think they are helping when they do things for them. But sometimes, the best way to be supportive is by being non-supportive.

If more wives would leave problem drinkers in the early stages of their drinking, their dependency on alcohol might end quicker and more marriages might be saved. If more alcoholics lost their jobs or careers in the early stages of their drinking, the shock might cause them to straighten up faster. If more alcoholics were left in jail longer after an accident or a DUI, they might realize quicker, that they are headed for trouble. The point is; the people who care about alcoholics wait too long before doing anything about it.

Being a good wife or husband doesn't mean you have to lie or cover up for an intoxicated spouse. It also doesn't mean that you or your children have to take physical and mental abuse from an intoxicated spouse. You may think that taking care of a spouse with a drinking problem makes you a noble character. But you're only prolonging the agony and you are not helping them.

Forget about the embarrassment and what people think! Deep down you are probably resenting what you are putting yourself through, and after the self-righteousness wears off, you will probably wind up hating yourself and them too.

The same thing applies to people who are trying to be a friend to someone with a drinking problem. Being a friend doesn't mean you have to be a schnook. But when you lend money to a drunk friend which he probably will not even remember, or lend him a car that might be wrecked, or take him into your home when he's been kicked out of his own, or recommend him for a job at your work place, a schnook is what you are. And if you think your alcoholic friend is going to be grateful for anything you do for him, you are sadly mistaken.

Parents, you have the greatest opportunity of all to save people from the hells of alcoholism, because you get the first opportunity. Being a good parent means recognizing and accepting the fact, that it is possible for anyone, of any age, class, creed, or color, to become an alcoholic. Being a good parent means, accepting the fact they do have a problem and getting them the help they need.

It has always amazed me, how the majority of people can't seem to accept the fact that alcoholics have the same desperation and depth of dependency as any other drug addict. They will go to the same lengths to support their habit as other drug addicts. And they will fight just as hard as any other drug addict to keep from doing anything about it.

How can one tell when a loved one is a potential alcoholic, or when they've had too much to drink? When a person goes through a complete personality change after a few drinks, then a few drinks is too much for them. If they drink often, have blackouts, and can't remember what they did after drinking, they are potential alcoholics. When you close your eyes and mind to the possibility of loved ones having a drinking problem, you are only postponing the inevitable. You are running the risk of most certain confinement, insanity, or death, to the ones you are trying to protect. You are also contributing to your loved ones making possible costly errors and having accidents that may cause serious injury to others.

Once a person's alcoholism has progressed beyond the point where loved ones can help, it becomes the problem of society as a whole and thus, the courts and the lawmakers. There are few laws now that provide any preventative measures, however, there could be.

People drink to excess to escape the pain, the fear, the reality and responsibility of life. Then wouldn't the greatest punishment and the ultimate rehabilitation be to pass laws that would place alcoholics and other drug abusers in the very context they sought to escape?

Consider the present situation. People, who were normally good, decent, intelligent and talented, people, before becoming alcoholics, are sent to prison for committing all types of crimes while intoxicated. In prison, they are forced to sober up because of the limited supply of booze. I say limited, because it has been proven that some alcohol and drugs are available in prison, provided you have the financial means to pay for them. While in prison, the state or government feeds and clothes them and they have no bills to pay. The remaining spouse, or relatives, or state and government agencies, such as Welfare and Aid to Dependant Children take care of their families. Bonding or insurance companies, possibly pay back the money they have embezzled or stolen. Insurance companies also pay for the automobiles they wrecked, the property they damaged, and even damages for the people they may have maimed or killed.

Even though they may be confined, they have escaped all the responsibility for the harm they caused. In prison, they have only themselves to look out for. And if they survive and behave themselves, they will eventually be back on the streets. But due to having a prison record, they will probably be unable to pursue their careers or work at their trade.

I have met former doctors who could no longer practice medicine. I have met former lawyers who could no longer practice law, former businessmen and women of all descriptions who could no longer engage in business. I have also met former artists, musicians, actors and performers of all types, who could no longer engage in their art and trades people of every description who could no longer practice their trade because they had records.

Most of these people had more anger, hated themselves more, and had more resentment and fear, than before going to prison. And upon release from prison, they now had to drink greater quantities and more often, in order to anesthetize the greater pain. Back on the streets, more than ever, these people are a dangerous threat to society.

Suppose laws were passed that even though confined, perpetrators would be forced to use their skills and talents by working outside the jail or prison or have work brought in to them. A portion of their earnings could be used to help support their families, a portion could go to the prison to help pay for their keep, and a portion could be used to repay the costs of whatever damage they caused. This type of a situation would make employers want to hire them when they were released. It would give the perpetrator the opportunity to continue to practice their profession or trade and upon release they would already be productive, useful citizens.

That type of situation would be punishment; it would be restitution; it would be rehabilitation; and it would be justice!

# Chapter 11

## CONCLUSION

Alcoholism is a terrible disease. It robs people of their health, happiness, integrity, dignity and their lives.. It also has an affect on all of the people who love, work with, associate with, and co-exist with alcoholics.

People drink alcoholic beverages because alcohol temporarily subdues the pain and fear of the realities of life. They become alcoholics without realizing it, because they become deluded by the false feeling of well being and invincibility that alcohol induces. Even when they finally realize they are addicted, they are slow to admit it and to seek help.

When, and if, they do stop drinking, they find that unfortunately, the same circumstances and situations they drank to escape from, still exist, along with all the other catastrophes that may have arisen because of their drinking. They also find that now, with a body weakened and ravaged by lack of nourishment and exercise, with a personality that has been twisted by lack of communication with others, and with a character that has little strength due to the lack of responsibility and ability to overcome adversity, they must face up to and overcome the same circumstances and situations they sought to escape.

Further, they will find little sympathy, forgiveness, or co-operation from the people they have wronged. They may, in fact, find that these people, who have left them alone when they were drunk, considering them hopeless, will come after them with a vengeance when they get sober, seeking restitution.

The truth is that recovering alcoholics will eventually have to be prepared to face up to everything sober that they failed to do, drunk. Alcoholism is only a postponement of the inevitable. The longer it is postponed the tougher it is.

The good news is that once people are able to overcome the madness of alcoholism and achieve the right quality of sobriety, they become much more stronger and useful people.

Perhaps the reason you haven't fit into a group is because you are a leader instead of a follower. Maybe you haven't fit into a religious environment because you're an atheist or agnostic but just haven't admitted it. It could be that you haven't responded to psychiatric treatment because you may have, through living experience, learned more about human nature than the psychiatrist you consulted. It is possible you haven't responded to group therapy because you are ironic. All of the above applied to me and my own dilemma in finding a way I could get sober and stay sober. So don't give up. Don't ever give up.

If you are able to stop drinking, by yourself, cold turkey, without medication, without group involvement, and without psychiatric treatment or therapy, the way I did, you will be able to stay sober in spite of ANYTHING. I have had many more trials and tribulations as a sober, responsible person, than I ever had as a drunk. I've even made some of the same mistakes. But sober, I allowed myself to feel the pain. I faced up to it and dealt with it. Obviously, the pain didn't kill me. In fact, it made me much stronger. The only effect that rejection, disappointment, and failure have on me now is to make me more determined. Sober, I am able to see my role in all situations and know that if it doesn't work out it is something I did or didn't do, that caused the problem.

I now devote my full time to writing and I write exclusively on speculation. I write books, screenplays, television movies, articles, short stories, songs and poetry. Some of these projects have taken me months, even years to complete. If you don't think it really hurts to send out something you've put a lot of time and effort into, and have it rejected by some publisher who barely glances at it and returns it with a form letter or doesn't even bother to respond at all, try it sometime.

When I was a drunk, such an incident would have been good for at least a two or three day binge. But now that I can think rationally, I know I either sent it to the wrong publisher, my timing wasn't right, or I simply didn't write good enough. But I don't give up. Even at my age I NEVER give up. I am always optimistic that eventually some of my material is going to succeed. I'm not projecting the outcome for I have no idea which of my properties will be successful, nor do I even care which one it will be. And the only person in the whole world, who believes it will happen, is me.

That is the attitude you must take when you make the choice to stop drinking cold turkey and on your own. No one is going to believe you can do it, but you...and now, me.

The truths pointed out in this book can be easily substantiated by anyone who will take the time to spend an afternoon in their local library and on the internet. The Book of Vital Statistics, the Almanac and The Business Abstract, will provide information about how much money is generated by the alcoholic beverage businesses and related businesses, how many people are employed in these businesses and the amount of taxes the Government collects annually from these businesses and their employees. You can also find out how much advertising money is spent and in which media, by the alcoholic beverage business.

You can find approximate figures on how many

alcohol-related crimes are committed, which though as staggering as it may seem, is nowhere near an accurate figure, in the Almanac.

You can find the information about the alcohol related deaths and injuries on the Health website of any computer.

Even though they are lax about informing the public about the contents and harmful effects of alcoholic beverages the media is the greatest source of information about the horror of alcoholism just by reporting the daily news. The media is also the best proof of the lengths the advertising agencies go to in enticing people to drink. During the same televised sporting event, you may see one of the watered-down, public service announcements against drunk drivers, followed by several ads for some brand of beer.

The contents of alcohol and its uses can be found in the dictionary.

The components, properties, and the effects of alcoholic beverages upon the mind and body can be found in the dictionary, Roget's thesaurus, and in any chemistry book.

The conclusions that came from the compiling of these facts cannot be found in other publications because the conclusions are my own.

I have told you the truth about alcohol, some of its harmful contents, its effects on the human mind and body, and the reasons for it being advertised, sold, and socially condoned. I have also told you the truth about yourself and your own power to do something about your own drinking problem. In addition, I have told you the truth about your being of value and being needed. It is not only important to YOU that you become sober and survive, it is imperative to the common good of the human race that you survive.

It is tragic that people can lawfully manufacture, advertise and sell a potentially dangerous product to fellow human beings without advising them of the contents and possible harmful side effects.

It is tragic for a government to condone the advertising and sale of such products to its citizens, and even conspire to cover up the possible danger and harm, for economic reasons.

And it is for sure tragic for so many people to die from diseases or accidents caused by the consumption of bottled and canned insanity, not having been advised on how it can and does destroy them.

Alcoholism is tragic! It is time for some serious changes in our system.

# THE END?

# Author's Notes

When I first began this book, because it was so personal, I never intended for it to ever be read by anyone except me. At the time, I was still active in the entertainment business and few people were even aware that I ever had a drinking problem. During subsequent years I have attempted to abandon the book many times, while I pursued more lucrative projects. However, for some reason, I found myself drawn back to it, time after time, always editing and making verbal corrections.

At one point, a literary agent presented the book to three large publishers without success. One of them called my agent and stated to him that even though he would be afraid to publish it, HE HAD stopped drinking after reading it.

I had abandoned all hope of ever getting the book published and put it at the bottom of my priority list until recently, when my interest was revived. Now finally, after all of these years, I have the opportunity to get this information to the public. I hope that many troubled people will find it to be helpful.

# Acknowledgements

I wish to thank my wife, who for fifty-five years has always been loyal, steadfast and true and has always believed in me, no matter what.

I wish to thank the people who shared their painful heartbreaking experiences with me.

I wish to thank the many librarians who helped me with my research.

Finally, I wish to thank Almighty God, who even though I denied His existence for the majority of my life, has demonstrated time after time with what can only be described as miracles, that He never denied me.

Printed in the United States
81649LV00001B/91